# JUSTICE FOR
# BABY ROSTON

by

Robert A. Anderson, Sr.

**DORRANCE**
PUBLISHING CO
EST. 1920
PITTSBURGH, PENNSYLVANIA 15238

Dorrance Publishing Co
585 Alpha Drive
Pittsburgh, PA 15238
Visit our website at *www.dorrancebookstore.com*

ISBN: 979-8-8868-3202-0
eISBN: 979-8-8868-3775-9

To Grace, my loving wife and best friend for the past 50 years, who died September 19, 2022 during this book's publication process. You were my inspiration in all matters. May you meet and hold Baby Roston in heaven and kiss him for his parents Kody and Megan Hanson.

# "Justice for Baby Roston: Prologue"

This book chronicles the arrest and prosecution of Kody Hanson, a new father who was charged with felony child abuse and murder in the death of Roston Hanson, his seventy-seven day old son who died on April 8, 2015 at a hospital in Wichita, Kansas. It is a recount of a new father's real-life nightmare - being falsely accused of felony child abuse and murder where law enforcement investigators failed to conduct a complete criminal investigation and inaccurately advised other criminal investigators; law enforcement supervisors; the prosecutors and the court that the father had made an incriminating statement during his interrogation, that he threw his son to the ground.

An audio and video tape of that interrogation clearly shows that Kody Hanson never made any such statement to law enforcement investigators and forensic evidence, diagnostic testing and the neuropathology report requested by the coroner all showed that no injury occurred to Roston Hanson on April 7, 2015 as alleged by law enforcement investigators and the prosecutors.

From the arrival of Roston Hanson at a Wichita, Kansas hospital where he was flown from Jetmore, Kansas by a life watch fixed-wing airplane on April 7, 2015 until the case was submitted to a jury on December 9, 2016, a medical pediatric specialist who examined Roston Hanson upon his arrival at the hospital, criminal investigators, and eventually prosecutors all jumped to a false conclusion of guilt, which was not supported by available diagnostic testing and forensic evidence.

The coroner's office failed to use histology during the provisional autopsy conducted on April 9, 2015 to view the edges of Roston Hanson's skull fracture under a microscope to determine whether the skull fracture was an acute or fresh fracture or an old healing injury. The coroner failed to meet the minimum expectations of an autopsy or follow the standards of practice for a baby's autopsy.

According to data from the National Child Abuse and Neglect Data System (NCANDS), forty nine states reported a total of 1,585 children died from child abuse or neglect in 2015 in the United States. Roston Hanson of Jetmore, Kansas who died at age seventy-seven days on April 8, 2015 in a Wichita, Kansas hospital was alleged by the Kansas Attorney General's Office and the Kansas Bureau of Investigation (KBI) to be one of those 1,585 children who died from child abuse in 2015.

Because Kody Hanson was a Hodgeman County Deputy Sheriff at the time his son was flown to get treatment at a Wichita hospital and a pediatric specialist trained in child injuries suspected Roston Hanson's condition to be the result of child abuse, the Hodgeman County Attorney recused himself and asked the Kansas Attorney General's Office to accept assignment of the case on April 7, 2015 involving a fellow Hodgeman County employee to investigate whether felony child abuse had occurred against Roston Hanson by Kody Hanson in Jetmore, Kansas. The Kansas Bureau of Investigation (KBI) is a division of the Office of the Kansas Attorney General and it is led by a director appointed by the Attorney General. Upon its establishment in 1939 by the Kansas Legislature, the KBI was given statewide jurisdiction to assist local agencies in dealing with more mobile and complex criminal activity.

On April 8, 2015 when Roston Hanson passed away at the Wichita hospital, the Kansas Attorney General's Office and the KBI opened a murder investigation claiming that Roston Hanson's death resulted from suspected child abuse which they alleged occurred against Roston Hanson by Kody Hanson on April 7, 2015 between 12:00 P.M. and 3:00 P.M. while Kody Hanson was watching Roston at their home in Jetmore, Kansas. A CT scan taken of Roston Hanson's head on April 7, 2015 at the Wichita Hospital soon after his arrival, showed for the first time that Roston had a large skull fracture. Law enforcement investigators alleged that Roston sustained the large skull fracture earlier that day between the specific three hours when Roston's mother was home for lunch and Roston appeared to be healthy and the time Kody Hanson called 9-1-1 and texted Roston's mother at the hospital where she was working as a nurse.

*Justice for Baby Roston* discuss the traumatic birth, short life, and tragic death of Roston Hanson and the unjust prosecution of Roston's father, Kody Hanson, on charges of felony child abuse and murder. The book highlights law enforcement investigators' rush to judgement to clear a death case and charge a parent, Kody Hanson without having the final results of the autopsy or conducting a complete criminal investigation or considering all possible causes for Roston Hanson's skull fracture found for the first time by a CT scan taken on April 7, 2015.

When babies and young children who because of their age cannot communicate or explain how they were injured are brought to medical facilities to be examined and treated for those injuries some medical personnel assume without any supporting medical or diagnostic evidence that the injuries are acute or fresh conditions that occurred from neglect or child abuse.

Where trained medical personnel jump to inaccurate assessments of neglect and child abuse or are misinformed by law enforcement personnel that a parent advised during his interrogation that he had thrown his baby to the ground and fail to use or consider the results of available diagnostic testing and forensic evidence which can determine whether an injury is an acute or fresh injury or an old and healing fracture and where coroners and other forensic experts fail to use histology during a provisional autopsy or meet the minimum expectations of an autopsy or follow the standards of practice for a baby's autopsy then parents, caregivers and others risk being falsely accused of neglect, felony child abuse and murder in unexplained and untimely baby death cases.

In any baby death case it is important for law enforcement investigators, pediatric specialists at hospitals and medical clinics and prosecutors to understand which diagnostic tests can be read by a radiologist who is trained in child trauma to date and determine whether a skull fracture found for the first time after a diagnostic CT scan of the baby's head is taken, is an acute and fresh injury or an old healing fracture. This is especially important when law enforcement investigators and prosecutors are claiming that the skull fracture occurred during a specific three-hour period earlier in the day before the baby was transported to the hospital and the diagnostic CT scan of Roston's head was taken within hours of the baby's arrival at the hospital.

One of the universal caveats of life is that there is nothing more painful to parents than the death of their child. Most parents pray to God that they live a long and healthy life and that their child or children are healthy and safe so that as parents they will never have to bury one of their children. A few parents who suffer the loss of a baby from an unexplained and untimely death are also falsely accused each year of causing their child's death from neglect or child abuse. Kody Hanson was one of those falsely accused parents in 2015. At the conclusion of this book, in chapter twenty, I make eighteen specific recommendations on how law enforcement investigators and their supervisors, medical personnel, forensic pathologists, coroners, prosecutors, and state legislatures can help keep parents from being falsely accused of neglect and child abuse in an unexplained and untimely death of a baby under similar circumstances which were faced by Kody Hanson in 2015.

# Chapter One:
## The Birth of Roston Hanson

On January 22, 2015 Roston Hanson was born by an emergency Cesarean Section (C-Section) surgical delivery at a Garden City, Kansas hospital which was necessary because the baby's mother's prolonged labor and her failure to progress. Prolonged labor, also known as failure to progress, occurs when labor lasts for approximately twenty hours or more for a first-time mother or fourteen hours or more if a mother has previously given birth. Roston's mother during her first pregnancy was in labor for over thirty-nine hours. She was in labor for twenty-seven hours after her membrane broke before the emergency C-Section was performed. She never dilated more than five centimeters. A ten centimeter dilation is required for a natural childbirth and vaginal delivery.

A C-Section is a surgical delivery of a baby usually performed when vaginal delivery poses a risk to the mother or baby. It is a surgical procedure used to deliver a baby through incisions in the abdomen and uterus. According to the defense OB/GYN (obstetrician-gynecologist) medical expert's trial testimony, emergency C-Section deliveries are normally preformed no later than twenty-four hours after a mother's membrane has broken to avoid potential injury to an unborn child or the mother.

Roston's mother testified at trial that she was told by her OB/GYN in the recovery room minutes after her emergency C-section that her baby was never going to pass through her birth canal because her baby's head was stuck in her birth canal and he had to reach in during the C-section and physically dislodge the baby's head. A picture taken in the recovery room by Kody Hanson a proud and loving new father within ten minutes of the C-section showed that Roston Hanson had a very pronounced elongated head.

Roston's parents were told prior to their baby's discharge from the hospital on the third day after the C-section by the surgical team's pediatrician that Roston was born with acid reflux and it would be necessary for a special feeding routine to be used to ensure that Roston was able to digest and keep formula down and to get enough nutrition and fluids from his feedings. Roston's parents were not told by the hospital or any of the three physicians involved in the C-section delivery of Roston Hanson or provided with any medical reports during the hospital stay or at discharge to suggest Roston was born with any birthing injury.

Roston's parents did not see the medical records listing that Roston Hanson was born with a birthing injury until after Kody Hanson's April 15, 2015 arrest and a request for medical records was sent to Roston's mother's OB/GYN. The receipt of the neuropathologist's report on October 6, 2015 of her forensic examination of Roston Hanson's brain, eyes, dura, and spinal cord showed that there was no injury to Roston that occurred on April 7, 2015 as alleged by the KBI investigators and the prosecutors. The neuropathologist was requested to complete a neuropathology examination by the Deputy Sedgwick County Coroner who performed the provisional autopsy of Roston Hanson on April 9, 2015 and observed brain damage that she did not recognize from other baby autopsies she had performed

# CHAPTER TWO:
## ROSTON'S INABILITY TO DIGEST FORMULA

At home, on road trips, at a relative's home and at his parents' friend's home, Roston had multiple incidents of projectile vomiting during his two and a half months of life. Roston's mother took Roston to his pediatrician on several occasions with her concerns that Roston had multiple episodes of projectile vomiting and was unable to keep his formula down. Projectile vomiting in infants can be caused by acid reflux but is most often due to a condition called pyloric stenosis. This condition affects a tube in the child's body that connects the small bowel and the stomach. Pyloric stenosis makes it difficult for an infant to get enough nutrition and fluids.

Projectile vomiting is a type of severe vomiting in which stomach contents can be forcefully propelled several feet away from you. It usually comes in shorter, more violent bursts than other types of vomiting. It is also more likely that projectile vomiting will come on suddenly with little or no warning. On April 5, 2015, during Roston's last office visit with his pediatrician just three days before Roston died on his seventy-seventh day of life, the pediatrician recommended to Roston's mother that because Roston was unable to keep his formula down that cereal should be added to and mixed with his formula before each feeding.

# Chapter Three:
## Roston's Aspiration and Resuscitatiion

On April 7, 2015, Kody Hanson was following the pediatrician's recommended special feeding procedure with his son, when Roston aspirated on his mixture of formula and cereal. Roston was fed one half of a five ounce bottle for the first time with the pediatrician's recommended mixture of formula and cereal by Kody Hanson while he was watching Roston at their home in Jetmore, Kansas. Roston aspirated during his feeding and Kody Hanson called 9-1-1 and texted his wife at the local hospital where she was working as a nurse.

The doctor from the local hospital and several nurses who worked with Roston's mother at the hospital drove their private vehicles to the Hanson home rather than waiting on an ambulance. In many small Western Kansas communities, the local volunteer fire department maintains the ambulances, and volunteer Emergency Medical Technicians (EMTs) are assigned each day to be on-call and carry a pager with them at all times they are on-call. When the on-call EMTs and volunteer firemen receive a page concerning an emergency and the need for an ambulance they have to travel from their home, work, or current location to the fire station to pick up the ambulance and then drive the ambulance to the location of the emergency. In most small towns and communities in Western Kansas, there are no full-time paid EMT employees who are standing by at a fire station like the larger cities have.

The Hodgeman County Sheriff whom Kody Hanson worked for as a Hodgeman County Deputy Sheriff drove to the Hanson home and he observed Kody Hanson coming from inside his house holding Roston in his arms and jogging towards him. Kody Hanson handed Roston to the nurses who had just arrived in the front yard of the Hanson home. The Sheriff testified at Kody Hanson's trial that Roston was, "Code blue, limp, unresponsive, and lifeless." The nurse handed Roston to the local doctor who had just arrived by private vehicle. The doctor began cardiopulmonary resuscitation (CPR) in the yard of the Hanson home and was able to resuscitate Roston after several minutes of CPR and Roston began breathing again on his own. CPR is a medical technique that is used to revive an individual from death.

The local doctor and a nurse and others present in the yard testified during the trial that a large amount of formula and cereal mixture was expelled from Roston's mouth during CPR. The doctor and later a nurse continued to perform CPR and removed additional formula and cereal mixture from Roston's mouth by use of their fingers while Roston was being driven by a private vehicle to the local hospital where Roston was examined, treated, and stabilized by the local doctor.

The local doctor from the Jetmore hospital determined that Roston would get better medical care by a larger hospital. The Garden City hospital where Roston was born seventy-six days earlier was contacted and they advised that they were not in a position to treat Roston. Roston was then taken by ambulance to the Jetmore, Kansas airport and flown by a fixed wing medical transport plane to the Wichita, Kansas airport and then transported to a large Wichita, Kansas hospital by a waiting ambulance. Roston's mother flew with her son and Kody Hanson was driven to Wichita by a friend. Roston Hanson had three seizures during the one-hour flight from Jetmore, Kansas to Wichita, Kansas and was given sedation medication by the flight crew after each seizure.

# CHAPTER FOUR:
## ROSTON'S ADMISSION TO A WICHITA HOSPITAL
## AND HIS INITIAL DIAGNOSIS

At the Wichita hospital, Roston Hanson's admission records contained statements about his emergency C-section delivery and the fact that Roston's mother was in labor for thirty-nine hours. As a part of the first day's examination and treatment of Roston Hanson, a diagnostic CT Scan of Roston's head was taken and it showed that Roston had a large skull fracture. The initial medical records from the Wichita hospital's pediatric specialist on the care team contained the following statements: "There is no doubt in my mind that this child has been the victim of severe and repeated abusive trauma ... nursing reports to me that the dad stated that he threw the infant down very hard on the ground, which might explain the fracture."

# CHAPTER FIVE:
## KODY HANSON IS INTERVIEWED AND INTERROGATED

Shortly after arriving at the Wichita, Kansas hospital on April 7, 2015, Kody Hanson was asked to speak to an investigative team of a City of Wichita police investigator and a KBI Special Agent. Kody Hanson agreed and he was interviewed in the basement of the Wichita hospital. During the interview the investigators questioned Kody Hanson about what he was doing at his home in Jetmore, Kansas between the hours of 12:00 P.M. and 3:00 P.M. on April 7, 2015 when he was caring for his son Roston Hanson.

The first interview of Kody Hanson was only audio-taped. Having a video and audio tape recording of an interview or interrogation helps everybody in an investigation. It makes clear if there had been improper pressure exerted on a defendant, and it also protects the interviewing or interrogating officers from false claims that such pressure had been brought to bear. Later that night, the same investigators asked Kody Hanson to speak with them again. Kody Hanson agreed with their request and he was taken to the Exploited and Missing Children's Unit (E.M.C.U.) building in downtown Wichita, Kansas where he was interrogated, after being advised of his Fifth Amendment Miranda rights.

Under Miranda v. Arizona, 384 U.S. 436 (1966), the United States Supreme Court ruled that the Fifth Amendment to the United States Constitution prevents prosecutors from using a person's statements made in response to an interrogation in police custody as evidence at their trial unless they can show that the person was informed of the right to consult with an attorney before and during questioning; the right against self-incrimination before police questioning and that the defendant not only understood those rights, but voluntarily waived those rights before answering any questions.

Police are required to inform anyone in police custody suspected of having committed any crime who is about to be interrogated, that: (1) "You have the right to remain silent; (2) Anything you say can be used against you in a court of law; (3) You have the right to an attorney and to have him or her present during the interrogation; and (4) If you cannot afford a lawyer, one will be appointed to you free of charge." The police investigator must also establish that the person being interrogated is voluntarily waiving those rights. This is normally established by having the person being interrogated sign a written waiver of rights, acknowledging that they understand their rights and waives them and by audio and video tapping the entire interrogation to include advising the defendant of his or her Fifth Amendment Miranda rights prior to starting an interrogation.

The interrogation was audio and video-taped. Kody Hanson was told by investigators that the doctors had determined that Roston Hanson had a large skull fracture and that those doctors had told the investigators that, the amount of force necessary to cause such a skull fracture would be equivalent to, "A fall from six stories or from a high impact auto accident." Kody Hanson told the investigators that he was unaware that Roston had a skull fracture and that Roston had not fallen six floors or been involved in any accident of any kind.

The investigators told Kody Hanson six different times during his interrogation that his son was upstairs in the hospital being worked on by doctors who were trying to save his son's life and that the doctors needed to know exactly what happened at his home in Jetmore, Kansas on April 7, 2015 between 12:00 P.M., the time when Roston's mother was home for lunch and Roston appeared to be healthy, and 3:00 P.M., when Kody Hanson called 9-1-1 and texted his wife at her work.

An investigator asked Kody Hanson during his interrogation if he was sure he didn't throw or drop Roston to the ground in frustration because Roston was crying and nothing Kody Hanson attempted caused Roston to stop crying. KBI special agents alleged in reports and through their interrogation questions that

Kody Hanson was stressed out because Roston Hanson was crying and nothing Kody Hanson tried to do would calm Roston down. Investigators suggested that Kody Hanson couldn't handle the stress and had snapped.

Kody Hanson testified at his trial that he was also a member of the Kansas Army National Guard at the time and had been deployed as a Kansas Army National Guardsman on two prior occasions to combat zones in Iraq and the Horn of Africa. Kody Hanson advised the investigators that he did not have any history of or any medical records of suffering from Post-Traumatic Stress Disorder (PTSD), or other medical conditions while serving in the Kansas Army National Guard or as a civilian police officer for two different Kansas police departments.

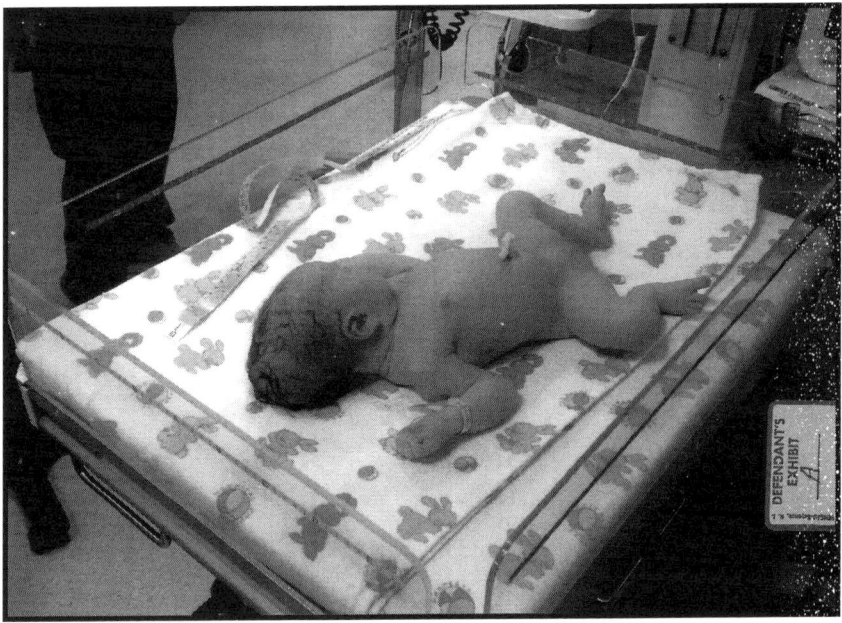

Copy of photo of Roston Hanson taken by his father, Kody Hanson on January 22, 2015 in the recovery room of the hospital within 10 minutes of Roston's emergency Cesarean surgical delivery showing his elongated head.

Kody Hanson's defense medical expert testified at the jury trial on December 8, 2016 that the large skull fracture was located directly under the elongated shaped portion of Roston Hanson's head shown in the picture taken by his father within ten minutes of his emergency C-section delivery. The eight and a half by eleven-inch color photograph of Roston Hanson taken after his emergency C-section birth showing the elongated head was marked as a defendant's exhibit, admitted, and published to the jury during my cross-examination of the state witness, the OB/GYN who delivered Roston Hanson by an emergency C-section.

When an admitted exhibit is published to the jury during the trial, it is handed to the jury and each jury member while they are in their seats in the jury box in the courtroom, takes the opportunity to view and examine the exhibit and then passes the exhibit to the next jury member until everyone on the jury has viewed the exhibit. Later on, when both sides have rested and the jury is given the instructions by the judge and sent back to the jury room to begin their deliberations the jury is given all of the admitted exhibits to have in the jury room during the jury deliberations.

When that photographic exhibit was observed with a magnifying glass (which all jurors, the OB/GYN witness and all legal counsel used to view the defendant's exhibit), there is a clear indentation on the side of Roston Hanson's head the same size and shape that forceps could make, based upon the courtroom drawing made by the OB/GYN witness at my request prior to showing the photograph to the witness, to show the jury the size and shape of the ends of forceps, a surgical instrument sometimes used to assist in some difficult emergency C-Sections.

The courtroom drawing of the size and shape of the end of the forceps the OB/GYN witness made was also marked as a defense exhibit and admitted by the court. At the end of the trial, the magnifying glass was also sent back to the jury room with all of the admitted exhibits. After Kody Hanson's interrogation, a KBI special agent told Roston Hanson's mother that Kody Hanson had acknowledged partial responsibility for Roston Hanson's injury. A review of the video and audio tape of Kody Hanson's interrogation shows that the statement by the KBI special agent that Kody Hanson had acknowledged partial responsibility for Roston Hanson's injury was a mischaracterization and not accurate.

# Chapter Six:
## The MRI Scan

On April 8, 2015 a diagnostic MRI (Magnetic resonance imaging) of Roston Hanson's head was also ordered by Roston Hanson's treating physicians at the Wichita hospital after the diagnostic CT-scan of Roston Hanson's head taken on April 7, 2015 showed Roston had a large skull fracture.

The MRI provides precise details of a person's body parts, especially soft tissue, with the help of magnetic fields and radio waves. An MRI may diagnose traumatic brain injury. A radiologist interprets the results of an MRI and classifies it as normal, abnormal, or potentially abnormal. An impression is provided based on the medical history and tests results. In case of ambiguity, possible diagnosis (differential diagnoses) are listed.

The MRI should have been read by a radiologist experienced in child trauma to determine from a reading of the MRI, if the skull fracture was a fresh or acute injury based upon whether there was fresh blood and sufficient swelling near the skull fracture or whether the skull fracture was an old, healing fracture. It is unknown whether the State had a radiologist experienced in child trauma read the MRI to explain those results to the prosecutors or criminal investigators.

The trial record and the reports filed by the criminal investigators suggest the KBI investigators failed to consult with a radiologist or have a radiologist experienced in child trauma read the MRI. The KBI special agents should have been consulted by the radiologist and told there was no fresh blood or sufficient swelling around the skull fracture which would have indicated that

Roston Hanson's skull fracture did not occur as alleged by law enforcement investigators between 12:00 P.M. and 3:00 P.M. on April 7, 2015 in Jetmore, Kansas when Roston Hanson was in his father's care.

The KBI special agents and the prosecutors should have asked the radiologist during their investigation of the death of Roston Hanson what the MRI showed in regards to dating the skull fracture of Roston Hanson. According to Dr. Evan Geller, Chief Editor of Medscape (2017): "The MRI is useful for detecting small, extra-axial fluid collections; early global ischemia, and shear injury, which may be missed on CT Scans. An MRI also aids in dating hemorrhage, depending upon the blood products present in the collections. Diffusion-weighted images are useful in detecting early ischemia. The MRI is superior to CT Scanning for differentiating hypo-attenuating subdural hemorrhage from prominent extra cerebral spaces of infancy."

The MRI was the medical evidence used during the jury trial by Kody Hanson's medical expert that showed the jury through a power point slide presentation of the MRI films, that there was no new blood or sufficient swelling around the large fracture which was proof that Roston Hanson's skull fracture did not occur on April 7, 2015 between 12:00 P.M. and 3:00 P.M., as alleged by the KBI investigators and the Kansas Attorney General's Office assigned to prosecute Kody Hanson.

The Assistant Kansas Attorney General Prosecutors elected months before the jury trial started to exercise their right to a Daubert Hearing prior to the defense medical expert's testimony. A Daubert Hearing is an evaluation by a trial judge on the admissibility of defined "expert," or scientific and technical testimony and evidence. The Daubert Hearing is conducted out of the jury's presence and is usually based on a motion in limine, which occurs before the trial even begins and determines which evidence or testimony will be presented to the jury. It is most efficient if the Daubert motion takes place after the discovery phase, so the hearing is completed before the trial starts.

The defense medical expert was required to appear from his home state by video conference where he was sworn in and the prosecutors were able to ask the defense medical expert about his qualifications as a medical doctor, his experience as a medical expert witness in various state and federal courts trials and his expert opinion that he formed after reviewing the medical records of Roston Hanson, the picture taken of Roston Hanson by Kody Hanson within ten minutes of the C-section, the CT Scan, the MRI film, and the neuropathologist's report.

The Hodgeman County District Court trial judge found the defense medical expert to be a qualified medical expert whose expert medical opinion could be offered as evidence at Kody Hanson's jury trial. The defense medical expert testified at Kody Hanson's jury trial on December 8, 2016 consistent with his testimony and answers given during the video conference Daubert Hearing held months prior to the jury trial. If the prosecutors had any medical expert whose interpretation of the MRI was different than the defense medical expert's interpretation of the MRI film they didn't produce such an expert at trial.

The State of Kansas did not call any radiologist experienced in child trauma in the State's case in chief, or call any medical expert as a rebuttal witness to attack or challenge the testimony of Kody Hanson's defense medical expert or the defense theory that the skull fracture was a birthing injury and did not occur on April 7, 2015 as alleged by the KBI investigators and the prosecutors. The defense medical expert opined that the skull fracture found on April 7, 2015 actually occurred during a difficult emergency C-section when Roston's head was stuck in his mother's birth canal and had to be physically removed by the doctor performing the C-Section. The defense medical expert testified that the skull fracture was immediately under the elongated portion of Roston Hanson's head and the brain damage to the subdural membrane that the neuropathologist found and opined in her report that it may actually represent resolving birth related trauma, was immediately under Roston Hanson's skull fracture.

# Chapter Seven:

## Kody Hanson's Parental Rights are Suspended by Local Law Enforcement Officers Based Upon Suspicion of Child Abuse

On April 8, 2015, Roston Hanson's condition worsened and local law enforcement officers advised Kody Hanson that his parental rights were being suspended based upon suspected child abuse. Kody Hanson was removed from Roston Hanson's intensive care unit (ICU) room and told he could no longer be in the same room with his son.

Roston's mother was advised that Roston may not survive the night and after consultation with the physicians at the Wichita hospital, a decision was made not to continue keeping Roston alive by artificial means and all life sustaining medical apparatuses were removed. Roston Hanson passed away on April 8, 2015 in the Wichita, Kansas hospital while his mother was present holding Roston's hand and Kody Hanson was speaking to his son Roston by telephone from outside the hospital room to Roston's mother's cellular telephone that she held to Roston's ear.

# Chapter Eight:

## The Deputy County Coroner
### Conducted a Provisional Autopsy

On April 9, 2015, the Deputy Sedgwick County Coroner conducted a provisional autopsy of Roston Hanson. The deputy coroner testified at the preliminary hearing held on December 22, 2015 that there was nothing from her April 9, 2015 provisional autopsy of Roston Hanson that showed Roston Hanson suffered any injury on April 7, 2015 as alleged by the KBI Special Agents and the prosecutors. An autopsy is a detailed dissection of a deceased person, done to determine why they died. Autopsies provide useful information about how, when, and why someone died. The Deputy Sedgwick County Coroner failed to use histology during the April 9, 2015 provisional autopsy, which would have disproved the state's theory that child abuse caused Roston Hanson's skull fracture on April 7, 2015 between 12:00 P.M. and 3:00 P.M. when Kody Hanson was alone with Roston Hanson at their home in Jetmore, Kansas.

At least one of the KBI Special Agents was present during the provisional autopsy of Roston Hanson conducted on April 9, 2015, after which the Deputy Coroner submitted a Provisional Anatomic Diagnosis on April 28, 2015. The KBI Special Agent would have been able to observe everything that the deputy coroner did and did not do during the provisional autopsy of Roston Hanson. The KBI Special Agent would have been able to observe the Deputy Sedgwick County Coroner view all the broken bones noted during the provisional autopsy under a microscope (a histology examination) other than the skull fracture observed for the first time on April 7, 2015 on the diagnostic CT scan of Roston Hanson's head and later read in the provisional autopsy report that those other broken bones were all old healing fractures and not fresh or acute fractures.

The practice of histology involves using a light or electron microscope to study cells and tissues of plants and animals. The only way to determine whether a fracture is a fresh or acute injury or an old healing fracture is to use histology and view the edges of skull fracture under the microscope.

If the KBI Special Agent was not aware that the only way to date a skull fracture is to use histology and view the edges of the skull fracture under a microscope to determine if it was a fresh or acute fracture, he should have asked the deputy coroner if she could determine whether or not Roston Hanson's skull fracture occurred on April 7, 2015 as the KBI special agents and the prosecutors had alleged. If the KBI Special Agent was already aware that the only way to date a skull fracture is by the use of histology during the autopsy, i.e. to view the edges of the skull fracture under a microscope to date the skull fracture and to determine if it was a fresh and acute fracture or an old healing fracture, he should have asked the Deputy Coroner to use histology and view the edges of Roston's skull fracture under the microscope.

If the Sedgwick County Deputy Coroner had viewed the edges of Roston Hanson's skull fracture on April 9, 2015 and determined that the skull fracture was an old healing fracture and not a fresh or acute fracture that occurred on April 7, 2015 as alleged by the KBI and Kansas Attorney General's Office and also had a radiologist, experienced in child trauma, read the April 8, 2015 MRI to date the skull fracture then the State of Kansas should not have filed the criminal charges against Kody Hanson on the state's theory that fatal child abuse occurred on April 7, 2015 in the home of Kody Hanson between 12:00 P.M. and 3:00 P.M. while Kody Hanson was caring for his seventy-six day old son.

The Deputy Coroner's provisional autopsy report and the letter she sent to a neuropathologist along with Roston Hanson's brain, eyes, dura, and spinal cord because the Deputy Coroner did not recognize the damage she observed to Roston Hanson's brain during the April 9, 2015 provisional autopsy, specifically lists: "Medical records indicate that the father threw his son to the ground."

The provisional autopsy report was received on April 28, 2015, two days before the Deputy Attorney General filed a pleading with the Hodgeman County District Court, in Jetmore, Kansas entitled: "Request to Submit Amended Affidavit and for an Additional Determination of Probable Cause." Whether the Deputy Sedgwick County Coroner assumed that the skull fracture occurred on April 7, 2015, as alleged by the KBI Special Agents, it was based upon the inaccurate statement in the medical records that the father allegedly said that he threw his son to the ground and did not use histology during the provisional autopsy to view the edges of the skull fracture under the microscope for that reason is unknown. It is also unknown whether the state during the prosecution of Kody Hanson ever had a radiologist, experienced in child trauma, read the MRI to date Roston Hanson's skull fracture.

# Chapter Nine:

## A KBI Special Agent Misled a Pediatric Specialist
## and the District Court Trial Judge

The pediatric specialist from the Wichita hospital where Roston Hanson passed away on April 8, 2015 testified at the preliminary hearing that the lead KBI Special Agent who was in charge of the investigation into the death of Roston Hanson (who by his own admission during his trial testimony was not present during either of Kody Hanson's interview or interrogation by the City of Wichita Police Investigator and other KBI Special Agents and he never viewed and listened to the audio and video-taped interrogation) told her on April 8, 2015 that Kody Hanson said during his interrogation that he had thrown Roston Hanson to the ground.

On April 10, 2015, a standard staffing meeting which is scheduled after the death of any child at their hospital was held at the Wichita hospital concerning the death of Roston Hanson. An employee with the Department of Children and Families (DCF) who participated in the staffing meeting by telephone from her office in Dodge City, Kansas while the medical personnel and law enforcement officers were present in person at the Wichita hospital, testified as a defense witness at Kody Hanson's jury trial that she heard and took notes when a law enforcement officer at that staffing meeting told those present and those participating by telephone that, "Kody Hanson had reached down and grabbed his son by the center and slammed him down. Up, overhead and down!"

On April 30, 2015, the Kansas Attorney General's Office filed a pleading entitled: "Request to Submit Amended Affidavit and for an Additional Determination of Probable Cause" in the Hodgeman County District Court. The state's pleading explained that the original affidavit of probable cause included a statement taken directly from the report of a physician at the Wichita hospital and that, since it was submitted, additional investigation has been completed which necessitates the clarification of the physician's original report. Specifically, the original statement that implied the defendant had stated to the nurses that the child had been thrown to the floor was incorrect. The pleading then explained that the information that the nurses apparently relayed to the Wichita hospital physician, in fact came from statements of the Defendant during his interrogation with a KBI Special Agent. This pleading was signed by the Deputy Attorney General.

I have over forty-two years of working in the criminal justice system. This includes ten years of experience as a law enforcement officer, detective, and lieutenant between 1970 and 1980. It also includes over thirty-two years as a licensed attorney in Kansas who represented indigent criminal defendants and retained criminal defendants between 1984 and 2016 on an estimated over 1,000 felony cases. During this time, I never saw any other pleading by a law enforcement agency, county attorney, or the KBI asking the trial judge to submit an Amended Affidavit and for an Additional Determination of Probable Cause in any of those cases or heard from other criminal defense attorneys that such a pleading was ever filed in one of their cases.

There were cases that were dismissed without prejudice to allow additional investigation and fact gathering before deciding to dismiss the charge or charges where there was false information contained in an affidavit of probable cause but that was very rare. There were also cases where the affiant law enforcement officer was found to have committed acts which were arguably criminal and any case where that law enforcement officer had filed an affidavit and the defendant's arrest was based solely on the affiant law enforcement officer's affidavit, all of his cases were dismissed by the county attorney because the law enforcement officer had been terminated for cause and would not have any credibility if any of his cases were contested and taken to trial. Normally under such circumstances, the criminal charge or charges, where there has been false testimony or false information contained in the affidavit of probable cause are dismissed by the prosecution and not refiled.

It is unknown whether the Deputy Attorney General viewed and listened to the interrogation of Kody Hanson which was both audio and video tapped or whether he assigned that task to a subordinate to determine whether Kody Hanson had said the alleged incriminating statement to the KBI Special Agent. A review of that video and audio tapped interrogation shows that Kody Hanson never told investigators that he threw his son Roston Hanson to the ground. The jury listened to and viewed on a large screen in the Hodgeman County District Court the complete audio and video tape of Kody Hanson's interrogation which was played during the state's case in chief at the jury trial.

If the Deputy Attorney General or his subordinate had actually viewed and listened to the audio and video-taped interrogation of Kody Hanson, and realized that the Attorney General's Request to Submit Amended Affidavit and for an Additional Determination of Probable Cause contained another false statement concerning whether Kody Hanson had told a KBI Special Agent during his audio and video taped interrogation that he had thrown Roston Hanson to the ground, he should have dismissed the charges filed against Kody Hanson without prejudice. He should have then ordered the KBI to conduct a complete criminal investigation into all possible causes of Roston Hanson's skull fracture to include a consultation with a radiologist from the Wichita hospital who had either read the diagnostic MRI or to have a radiologist experienced in child trauma read the diagnostic MRI taken on April 8, 2015 to find out whether the skull fracture observed for the first time by anyone on April 7, 2015 in the diagnostic CT scan was a fresh and acute fracture or whether it was an old healing fracture which did not occur on April 7, 2015 as alleged by the KBI Special Agents and the prosecutors.

A dismissal without prejudice means a case has been dismissed but has not been finally decided. If a case is dismissed without prejudice it may be refiled by the prosecution. If a case is dismissed and the court order is not specific with regards to prejudice, it is considered a dismissal without prejudice. A dismissal without prejudice is a proceeding that allows the prosecution to dismiss their charges against a defendant, which releases a defendant from custody if they are currently confined in jail, or releases a defendant from any bond conditions and allows the prosecution to continue to investigate the alleged crime and refile the same or other charges without having to defend against a defense claim of double jeopardy.

Double jeopardy is a procedural defense (primarily in common law jurisdictions) that prevents an accused person from being tried again on the same (or similar) charges following an acquittal. The double jeopardy clause in the Fifth Amendment to the U.S. Constitution prohibits anyone from being prosecuted twice for substantially the same crime. The lead KBI Special Agent assigned to investigate the death of Roston Hanson testified at trial that he did not review the video and audio tape of Kody Hanson's interrogation before charges of murder and felony child abuse were filed against Kody Hanson in the Hodgeman County District Court, Jetmore, Kansas.

# CHAPTER TEN:

## KODY HANSON CHARGED WITH MURDER AND
## FELONY CHILD ABUSE IN THE DEATH OF ROSTON HANSON

A local Wichita, Kansas attorney was retained and consulted with Kody Hanson on April 8, 2015. That retained attorney spoke with the original assigned Assistant Attorney General handling Kody Hanson's case and was told by her that no criminal charges would be filed until after the autopsy report was received. However, on April 16, 2015, Kody Hanson was arrested on charges of murder and felony child abuse and incarcerated.

On April 20, 2015 six months before the final autopsy reports were received from the deputy coroner, an affidavit and complaint were filed with the Hodgeman County District Court, Jetmore, Kansas charging Kody Hanson with murder, an off-grid felony and felony child abuse. I was court-appointed by the Hodgeman County District Court on April 30, 2015 after Kody Hanson's retained counsel who had filed a limited entry of appearance withdrew at the first appearance. A judge from the Hodgeman County District Court asked me to accept court-appointment as Kody Hanson's criminal defense attorney.

Kody Hanson remained in pre-trial confinement in four different county jails for over six months until the trial judge, over the objections of the state lowered Kody Hanson's bond to a $100,000 corporate surety bond with additional conditions that Kody Hanson at his own cost wear a GPS monitoring device and not leave a ten mile radius from where he would be residing and working. Bonding companies usually charge a fee of ten percent (10%) of the actual bond to sign for the whole bond in order to get a defendant released from jail and on bond during the pendency of any criminal case after charges have been filed and a bond has been set by the court. The bonding company doesn't have to post the full bond with the district court but is required to sign a promise to pay the full bond amount if the criminal defendant fails to show up in court or appear at any scheduled hearing when the defendant is released on bond. A bonding company is allowed to contest and have a hearing on any court order to revoke a criminal defendant's bond and order the bonding company to pay into court the full bond.

It cost Kody Hanson $10,000 (ten percent) of the actual bond amount, which he had to pay the bonding company as a non-refundable fee to be released on bond pending his jury trial. He also had to pay the cost of the court-ordered GPS monitoring while he remained released from jail and on bond. Those payments or fees are never recovered from the bonding company or GPS monitoring company even in cases where a criminal defendant is later acquitted of the charges.

# Chapter Eleven:

## Roston Hanson was Born with Birthing Injuries

After Kody Hanson's arrest and incarceration Roston Hanson's mother collected the medical records concerning Roston Hanson's birth from the Garden City Hospital and from her OB/ GYN's office. Those medical records listed that Roston Hanson was born with cephalohematoma, a birthing injury. "A cephalohematoma is a hemorrhage of blood between the skull and the periosteum of any age human, including a newborn baby secondary to rupture of blood vessels crossing the periosteum. The usual causes of a cephalohematoma are a prolonged labor or instrumental delivery, particularly forceps delivery. In some cases, it may be an indication of a linear skull fracture. Skull radiography or CT scanning is also used if concomitant depressed skull fracture is a possibility. (Wong, Chin-Ho, et. al., (2006). "Calcified Cephalohematoma: Classification, Indications for Surgery and Techniques." *The Journal of Craniofacial Surgery*)

Prior to the receipt of the autopsy reports on October 6, 2015, I attempted to meet with and speak to the three physicians who were involved in the C-section delivery of Roston Hanson. Each physician was sent a letter along with an eight and a half by eleven inch color copy of the picture of Roston Hanson taken by Kody Hanson within ten minutes of Roston Hanson's C-Section delivery, which showed Roston Hanson had a very pronounced elongated head.

The letter advised each of the physicians that I was the court-appointed defense attorney who was representing Kody Hanson who was charged in the Hodgeman County District Court with murder and felony child abuse in the death of his son Roston Hanson because a large skull fracture was found during a CT scan taken on April 7, 2015 at a Wichita, Kansas hospital. My letter suggested that the skull fracture may have occurred during the prolonged labor and the emergency C-section delivery of Roston Hanson when they were the attending physicians.

A letter was received within days of my letters being sent, from a Wichita, Kansas attorney, notifying me that he represented the Garden City Hospital where Roston Hanson was born and all three physicians that I had written and explaining that the three physicians were declining to meet with me and answer any questions about the birth of Roston Hanson. The attorney's letter did state that each doctor would appear and testify at Kody Hanson's court hearings if there were subpoenaed. The lead KBI Special Agent testified at the jury trial that he also attempted to speak with the three physicians involved in the C-Section delivery of Roston Hanson and was told that since their attorney would not allow them to speak with Mr. Hanson's attorney they would not agree to speak with the KBI Special Agent investigator.

On the day the KBI Special Agent was advised that the doctors would not agree to be interviewed by the KBI, the State of Kansas through the Kansas Attorney General's Office should have dismissed Kody Hanson's criminal charges without prejudice and immediately commenced an inquisition in the Hodgeman County District Court under a unique Kansas inquisition statute, K.S.A. 22-3101(1) and subpoenaed all medical records of Roston Hanson's mother and Roston Hanson and each of the three physicians, the surgical nurses and any inventory of surgical instruments used during the C-section and all other medical personnel present during the C-section delivery of Roston Hanson.

The Kansas Attorney General's Office had utilized a K.S.A. 22-3101(1) inquisition in another baby death case filed in the Ellsworth County District Court, Ellsworth, Kansas in 2014 prior to filing murder charges against a mother. The lead Assistant Attorney General assigned to that Ellsworth County case was the same Assistant Attorney General originally assigned to Kody Hanson's case. Despite the clear need and ability to force witnesses to appear before an inquisition court and answer the prosecutor's questions concerning the possible causes of

Roston Hanson's skull fracture and the statutory authority to utilize a K.S.A. 22-3101(1) inquisition, the State of Kansas never used the power of inquisition in their investigation of the death of Roston Hanson.

K.S.A. 22-3101 (1) authorizes the Kansas Attorney General, an assistant attorney general, the county attorney, or the district attorney of any court to apply to the district court to conduct an inquisition. Once an inquisition has been commenced by the Kansas Attorney General or assistant attorney general, a district attorney or county attorney, the attorney general, assistant attorney general or an assistant district or county attorney may question witnesses. In the Matter of the Investigation into the Homicide of T.H., 23 Kan.App.2d. 471, Syl. 5 (1997).

The Kansas Attorney General's Office and the Assistant Attorney Generals assigned to prosecute Kody Hanson were advised prior to their receipt of the autopsy and neuropathology report by written correspondence and in defense pleadings filed with the Hodgeman County District Court that the defense's theory was that Roston Hanson's skull fracture found for the first time on April 7, 2015 in a CT Scan and MRI taken on April 8, 2015 at the Wichita Hospital was a "birthing injury" caused by the prolonged labor of Roston Hanson's mother and that it did not occur on April 7, 2015 between 12:00 P.M. and 3:00 P.M. in Jetmore, Kansas, as alleged by the KBI and the prosecutors.

It was clear from the preliminary hearing testimony of the Deputy Sedgwick County Coroner, the Wichita hospital crisis team's pediatric specialist, and law enforcement officers that they were all made aware by the prosecutors of the defense's theory that Roston Hanson suffered a birthing injury. However, no apparent efforts to investigate whether Roston Hanson suffered a birthing injury were initiated by law enforcement, medical personnel, or the prosecutors other than the one-time unsuccessful attempt by the lead KBI Special Agent to speak to the OB/GYN and other attending physicians present during the C-section delivery of Roston Hanson.

# Chapter Twelve:

## Final Autopsy Report Received
## by the Kansas Attorney General's Office

On October 6, 2015, the State of Kansas received the final autopsy report of the Deputy Sedgwick County Coroner along with the additional neuropathology report. The coroner concluded that Roston Hanson's death was a homicide and listed blunt force trauma to the head as the cause of death. Homicide is an act of a person killing another person. The autopsy report stated that the deputy coroner viewed other broken bones - a left 6th rib fracture and a bucket handle fracture of the proximal left tibia under the microscope and opined that they were old healing fractures and not fresh or acute injuries.

"All babies suffer at least minor trauma, leading to bruising or swelling of the scalp, during a vaginal delivery. More serious injury can occur during a complicated delivery, particularly if the baby is too big to pass easily through the mother's pelvis. Broken bones, particularly ribs are a hazard of difficult deliveries. The bones usually heal easily." (The American Medical Association Encyclopedia of Medicine, p. 173)

The neuropathologist report stated that Roston Hanson had suffered a stroke (anoxic-ischemic encephalopathy) in-vitro (in the womb), during birth, or immediately after birth, which destroyed the frontal lobes of Roston Hanson's brain. The MRI taken on April 8, 2015 shows that no new bleeding or pathology of the brain was present and the pathology was already early subacute (three to seven days old) at the time of the MRI. The MRI showed the old brain damage from the stroke suffered by Roston Hanson in the womb, during the thirty-nine hours of his mother's prolonged labor or immediately after his birth, as opined by the neuropathologist.

The neuropathologist report did not suggest that Roston Hanson suffered any injury on April 7, 2015, as alleged by the KBI special agents and prosecutors. The neuropathology report stated: "The right parasagittal parietal lobe demonstrates a distinct lesion characterized by infiltration by mixed inflammatory infiltrates, including numerous macrophages indicating an insult at least two days removed" and "The present of frequent iron-positive siderophages and vascular proliferation increase the timeframe since insult at least three to seven days."

Concerning the examination of Roston's eyes the neuropathologist stated: "The iron positivity in frequent siderophages indicates a time frame of at least three days since the initial insult/injury. She concluded her report by stating: "Likewise, the subdural membrane is at least one week in formation, and may actually represent resolving birth related trauma."

The neuropathologist advised me during a consultation in her Tulsa, Oklahoma office that her examination of Roston Hanson's brain, eyes, dura, and spinal cord did not show that Roston Hanson suffered any physical injury on April 7, 2015 as alleged by law enforcement investigators and the prosecutors and that, "The only way to date a skull fracture during an autopsy was to use histology and view the edges of the skull fracture under a microscope."

During the jury trial the neuropathologist was called as a state's witness and acknowledged during her cross-examination by me, her statements made to me during our consultation in her office months earlier, which are described in the above paragraph. The defense's medical expert testified at trial that the subdural membrane discussed and described in the neuropathology report as being "at least one week in formation, and may actually represent resolving birth-related trauma" was located immediately under Roston Hanson's skull fracture seen on the April 7, 2015 CT Scan and April 8, 2015 MRI of Roston Hanson's head and skull fracture. The defense medical expert also testified at trial that the skull fracture was located immediately under the elongated portion of Roston Hanson's head that was caused from being stuck in the mother's birthing canal.

Once the State of Kansas received the autopsy report of the Deputy Sedgwick County Coroner and the report of the neuropathologist, the State of Kansas should have immediately dismissed the charges against Kody Hanson without prejudice and commenced an inquisition in the Hodgeman County District Court pursuant to K.S.A. 22-3101(1) and subpoenaed the physicians and nurses, the inventory of surgical instruments used during the delivery, and any other medical personnel present during the emergency C-section delivery of Roston Hanson.

That information includes the following: "Likewise the subdural membrane is at least one week in formation, and may actually represent resolving birth related trauma." This was clearly exculpatory evidence for Kody Hanson and should have been made a part of the complete criminal investigation of the death of Roston Hanson. Exculpatory evidence is evidence favorable to the defendant in a criminal trial that exonerates or tends to exonerate the defendant of guilt. It is opposite of inculpatory evidence which tends to present guilt. Once again, the State of Kansas failed to use the power of the inquisition, which under Kansas law was solely available to prosecutors, in their investigation of the death of Roston Hanson.

The KBI Special Agents who were responsible for the investigation into the death of Roston Hanson testified at the preliminary hearing held on December 8, 2015 that they had not been provided with a copy of the neuropathology report received by the State and the Kansas Attorney General's Office on October 6, 2015 nor did they know the contents of that report which suggested that Roston Hanson's brain injuries did not occur on April 7, 2015 as alleged by the State of Kansas and that the injuries were old healing injuries and may be resolving birth-related trauma, even though that neuropathology report had been in the State's custody and control for over two months prior to the KBI Special Agents sworn testimony at the preliminary hearing.

# Chapter Thirteen:
## The Jury Selection Process

Prior to the start of the jury trial, the pool of potential jurors was summoned to the court and questioned by both counsel for the state and counsel for the defendant, during the jury selection process called voir dire, which is French for "to speak the truth." It is the process through which potential jurors from the venire are questioned by either the judge or a lawyer to determine their suitability for jury service.

The main purpose of voir dire is to find out from the potential juror answers to the following general questions: (1) Whether they have a serious reason that prevents them from completing jury duty; (2) Whether they know any of the parties in the case; (3) Whether they have a financial interest in any of the parties in the case; and (4) whether they have a bias or prejudice that prevents them from being impartial jurors.

The trial judge authorized the defense request for an expanded jury questionnaire to be sent by the Clerk of the Court to all potential jurors who were issued notices to appear for jury duty at the Hodgeman County District Court, Jetmore, Kansas on November 26, 2016 and were instructed to complete and return the expanded jury questionnaire to the Clerk of the Court, weeks before the date they were instructed to appear for jury duty. This allowed both the attorneys for the state and defense to review the completed jury questionnaires prior to the start of the jury trial and voir dire process.

Expanded jury questionnaires which are much longer and more detailed than the standard jury questionnaires are very helpful to the process of determining whether any potential jurors have any bias or any association with law enforcement or prior jury service and allows the attorneys to get to know a juror and their thought process prior to the voir dire questioning.

The expanded jury questionnaires contain a number of personal questions that are not contained in the standard jury questionnaire. I found that by asking the potential jurors these personal questions in the jury questionnaire such as: What person in your life are you the proudest of and why?, the potential juror's answer gives me a better idea of how a particular juror thinks based upon their written answers and oral answers if I choose to follow-up with additional questions during voir dire. I also believe that such a process allows a potential jury member to feel, and rightfully so, that I am interested in them as a human being and not as a robot.

I always take most of those personal questions and answer them myself and tell the entire potential jury pool when I am first allowed to address the potential jurors during the voir dire proceedings that since I have asked them to give me answers to what could be considered as personal questions, that it is only fair if I provide the jury with my answers to some of those questions. I have found that giving the jurors my answers to the personal questions puts them at ease and more relaxed. It also starts a dialogue between me and the potential jurors and makes it easier to ask the jurors multiple questions.

In this jury trial, I used a jury consultant who was an expert in both non-verbal communications and on jury selection who reviewed the answers given in the jury questionnaires and who was also present during the voir dire jury selection process listening to the potential jurors' answers, and observing their body postures and facial expressions while other jurors are being questioned and when the individual juror is being questioned by the state and the defense.

There is a very complex scientific approach to selecting jurors. How a juror sits in the juror's chair, how a juror folds his or her arms and his or her facial expressions; and multiple other tells, all contain possible information about whether the potential juror is liberal or conservative, is open-minded or closed-minded, and whether they may be receptive to a client's defense.

For example, when a juror sits in the jury box and folds their arms it is thought that they may be closed minded and have already made up their minds and are not subject to being persuaded by the attorney speaking. However if that same potential juror uncrosses his or her arms and moves forward in their chair and appears to pay closer attention when either the prosecutor or defense counsel is asking questions for the first time, jury consultants suggest that such jurors are not closed minded and should take their oath very seriously and may tend to agree more with the party that is speaking at the time they unfolded their crossed arms and sat up in their chair.

The internet emerged in the United States in the 1970's but did not become visible to the general public until the early 1990's. In 1984, when I tried my first jury trial before there was any social media to research potential jurors' posts and the like, an attorney had to ask questions of potential jurors that were not on the jury questionnaires and have other individuals review the list of potential jurors to find out if anyone had any personal knowledge of any of the potential jurors. Now, jury consultants research the potential jurors on the internet and learn a lot about individual potential jurors by seeing their answers to expanded jury questionnaires and any social media posts they may have made.

It is important for a defense attorney to use a jury consultant during the voir dire jury selection process in a higher-level felony or off-grid felony so the jury consultant can watch all of the potential jurors and their body posture and body movement while the defense attorney concentrates on the individual potential juror that he or she is questioning and make brief notes from the answers received and from their observations. It is very important to compare notes between the defense attorney and the jury consultant so you can score the potential jurors to decide which jurors you want to challenge for cause and which jurors you might want to use one of the peremptory challenges to keep them off a particular jury and which jurors you hope will be selected for jury service by not being taken off during voir dire with a challenge for cause or a peremptory challenge by either the state or defense.

Past for cause means that you are satisfied with the potential juror and do not intend to attempt to have the juror removed from the potential jury pool for cause. If an attorney can get an unfavorable juror dismissed for cause then it benefits their client to have all of the peremptory challenges left to remove other jurors who you do not think based upon answers in the jury questionnaire and during voir dire would be a favorable juror for your client and that a challenge for cause may be unsuccessful.

The jury consultant I used in Kody Hanson's jury trial is a licensed attorney. I had used her months before in an off-grid felony jury trial and her assistance was very helpful. After Kody Hanson's jury trial, she was hired as a senior trial attorney by my oldest son who is a criminal defense attorney who worked for me and took over my office when I semi-retired and moved to Mississippi. I didn't start using a jury consultant until 2014 but I never tried any case where I was representing an indigent criminal defendant in an off-grid or other serious felony case after 2014 where I didn't seek approval from the trial court to use an expanded jury questionnaire and where I didn't hire and use a jury consultant to assist me in picking a jury. A jury consultant's services and their unique knowledge of non-verbal communications are very valuable to a criminal defense attorney's ability to pick jurors who are best suited for their client's defense.

It is also very important for a criminal defense attorney to have his or her client's involvement in the voir dire process by having them and their families observe the potential jurors and their answers, etc., and then consult with the lead defense attorney about any potential jurors that the client does not feel comfortable having on their jury. It is not uncommon if your client is a resident of the county where the criminal jury trial is being held to know one or more potential jurors. It is the client's trial and although the attorney is given a lot of latitude in deciding most trial decisions, the decision whether to testify in his or her own defense is the client's decision. Likewise, the client should be able to tell his or her attorney if they are uncomfortable with a specific potential juror and discuss those concerns with their attorney during the voir dire process.

The jury consultant I had hired noted from her initial review of the expanded jury questionnaires that three of the jury pool members were employed as physician assistants at medical facilities. In Western Kansas where the jury trial was held, physician assistants provide medical treatment to the majority of their small towns and local communities because there are not as many medical doctors in the rural areas of Kansas.

In Kody Hanson's jury trial medical knowledge was very important since the diagnostic tests given to Roston Hanson, a CT scan and an MRI test; the autopsy reports; the medical records and the medical expert testimony given during the jury trial were critical to the defense theory of the case and in my opinion fatal to the state's theory. I wanted to have at least one of the three physician assistants picked as a juror to bring their special medical knowledge to the jury room. I wanted to keep all three physician assistants from being excused or removed from the potential jury by the state using three of their peremptory challenges to remove all three physician assistants from the jury.

During my questioning of one of those three physician assistants during voir dire, I asked the trial judge to excuse her for cause because of the possible effect of being away from her patients for two weeks would prejudice the health of her community. The state objected to my request to have that potential juror excused for cause and after answering the state's follow-up questions and the trial judge's questions the first physician assistant was excused for cause by the trial judge due to the hardship it would cause her community members who relied on her for medical treatment and because the jury trial was expected to last two full weeks.

The state prosecutors struck one of the two remaining physician assistants with one of their peremptory challenges. I assumed but do not know that the State prosecutors believed given my objection and request to have one of the physician assistants removed for cause, that I would use one of the defendant's peremptory challenges to remove one of the two remaining physician assistants so there would not be any of the three physician assistants on the jury.

During the voir dire process, each side can challenge any of the potential jurors for cause but bears the burden of establishing that cause. After the potential jurors are passed for cause and remain in the potential panel of jurors, the prosecution and the defense each get a specific number of peremptory challenges of any potential jurors made as a right without assigning any cause. After both the state and defense made all of their challenges the remaining twelve jurors and two alternant jurors were impaneled for the start of the jury trial. All fourteen jurors appear each day of trial and the two alternant jurors are not chosen until both sides rest and right before the jury is sent by the trial judge to go back into the jury room and pick a foreperson and start deliberating the fate of the defendant.

All fourteen jurors' names are placed in a hat or box and the Clerk of the Court or bailiff is asked by the trial judge to reach into the raised hat or box and pick two names out of the hat. Those two names are the alternative jurors and do not retire at the end of the jury trial with the other twelve jurors to the jury room to start deliberating on the fate of the defendant. Having alternate jurors allows the jury trial to continue even if one of the jurors becomes ill or has a family emergency which necessitates his or her having to stop being a juror and return home for their family emergency. In any case where a juror has to stop being a juror because they become ill or they have a family emergency, the jury continues to appear each day with the remaining thirteen jurors.

If one of the jurors has to stop being a juror because they become ill or they have a family emergency when the jury trial is finished and the jury is deliberating, that juror is replaced by one of the alternative jurors. While such situations are rare, and I cannot recall that ever happening in any of my criminal jury trials, this process is a preventative measure that keeps a trial judge from having to declare a mistrial if the full statutory number of jurors (twelve in felony prosecutions and six in misdemeanor prosecutions) is not available to complete the jury trial and deliberate at the conclusion of the jury trial. The alternate jurors are instructed to remain at the courthouse when the jury is sent back to the jury room to begin deliberations. The alternant jurors are not released until the jury has reached their verdict.

One of the three physician assistants remained in the jury pool and was not removed by either the state or defense with a peremptory challenge. The defense was pleased with the remaining jurors and the exhaustive work the jury consultant had done. Mr. Hanson and I felt confident that he was going to get a fair jury trial. The attorneys do not know who the jury foreperson is during jury deliberations until the jury informs the trial judge that they have reached a verdict and the trial judge calls them back into the court to give their verdict and the trial judge asks them to identify their jury foreperson.

# Chapter Fourteen:
## Defense Closing Arguments

At the conclusion of the jury trial after both parties have rested the trial judge reads the agreed upon jury instructions submitted by the parties to the court and instructs the jury to pick a foreperson when they are sent back to the jury room to begin deliberating. The trial judge tells the jury that the state will be presenting closing arguments first because the state has the burden of proof and then the defense counsel will present closing arguments. Because the state has the burden of proof of beyond a reasonable doubt their attorney argues first, but reserves some of their allotted time to speak again at the end of the defense closing arguments.

The defense knows it will not be able to counter any argument the state makes in the state's second portion of their closing arguments unless what is being argued violates rules and then the defense counsel can lodge an oral objection at the time such argument is being made. The trial judge rules on the objection and if the trial judge sustains the objection, the trial judge instructs the jury to disregard whatever the state attorney said which was objected to. If the trial judge overrules the defense objection then the state attorney is allowed to continue arguing whatever they were saying at the time defense counsel objected. Attorneys must choose wisely when they are objecting because if their objection is not sustained by the trial judge, it could bring an emphasis to such argument and cause the jury to wonder why defense counsel was trying to keep something from the jury.

It is important for defense counsel to cover all areas that he or she believes the state may choose to argue in their arguments made during the time reserved for after the defense gives their entire closing argument. For that reason, I developed a habit of preparing my closing arguments in writing to read to the jury so that I wouldn't risk forgetting to discuss potential important facts or evidence during my one and only opportunity to speak to the jury. I prepare those written arguments prior to the last day of any jury trial and save them on my computer and if there is a need I edit them prior to giving my closing arguments in any jury trial.

The trial judge specifically informs the jury members that the closing arguments of the prosecution and the defense counsel are not evidence, but only arguments in support of their theories of the case. The trial judge also advises the jury that in a criminal case their verdict must be unanimous and all twelve jurors must find the defendant guilty for a guilty verdict. Below is the exact wording of some but not all of the defense written closing arguments I prepared and gave an oral presentation to the jury during my closing argument to the jury before the jury was sent to deliberate on whether Kody Hanson was guilty or not guilty:

"May it please the court, Ms._____, Ms._____ and ladies and gentlemen of the jury. First and foremost, let me on behalf of Kody Lee Hanson thank you for your service in this case as attentive jurors. I assure you that to Kody Lee Hanson there is nothing bigger and more important to finally be able to tell his side of this story and to present the actual medical evidence which has shown that Roston Hanson did not suffer a blunt force trauma or any injury on April 7, 2015 as alleged by the state. To you as the combined and individual jurors, it should also be an important civic responsibility to you to be here each day and to carefully listen to all of the evidence and judging by the way I have observed you all for the past 8 days it has been. All of you appear to have listened very carefully to all witnesses who presented sworn testimony from that stand.

Do you recall the voir dire process on Tuesday November 26, 2016 and the long series of questions I asked each of you both individually and as a group? Now is the time to act on those answers each of you gave. I asked each of you if there was evidence presented that tended to show that a crime may have been committed and there was also evidence that tended to show that no crime was committed, who would get the benefit of that doubt and whether your verdict would be guilty or innocent under those circumstances?

Each of you clearly indicated it would be 'innocent.' I also asked each of you whether you could be strong in your opinion and render a verdict that reflected how you interpreted the evidence and the facts and not be persuaded or influenced by others without careful consideration. Do you remember us having the conversation during voir dire that the American jurisprudence system is not one of the majority rules? Do you recall our conversation about if the tide was turned and you were facing criminal charges what you would both expect and hope that law enforcement would do in their investigation of the alleged crime to assure that you would receive a fair and impartial trial?

I have the following observation to make, the right to a fair trial is guaranteed - but the right to a fair investigation is not! The very limited investigation that was conducted before the investigating officer jumped to a conclusion should shock every one of your conscious. I am not suggesting that this is a case of police misconduct; rather, it is a clear case of police non-conduct.

Clearly I do not expect nor do I ask each of you to expect that there should have been a complete "C.S. I" investigation but I respectfully request that you as individuals and as a combined jury hold the state of Kansas to their burden of proof of beyond a reasonable doubt as you are required to do according to the jury instructions given to you by the Court.

When you first reported for jury duty, you were not asked to check your common sense and life experiences at the door and told by the Judge or bailiff not to use them. Rather you were instructed by the Court that you can and should use your life experiences and common sense in your deliberations. Please do use your common sense and your life experiences when you are sent back into the jury room for one last time and you pick a foreperson and start deliberating and judging the testimony of all witnesses and when deciding whether the State of Kansas has met their very strong burden of proof of proving each and every element beyond a reasonable doubt.

How many of you in seeing your own newborn babies or newborn babies of your children or friends have ever observed a newborn baby to have an elongated cone head? You saw the picture taken within ten minutes of Roston's emergency C-section birth and you heard Dr. Galaznik testify that the elongated head was directly over the skull fracture. What are the odds of this happening? Ask yourself, when Roston Hanson was born with cephalohematoma, a birthing injury that is often an indication of an underlying skull fracture according to Dr. Heflin and when Roston Hanson had a stroke in the womb; during his birthing process or immediately after birth that damaged the frontal lobes of his brain and given Roston's failing to keep formula down in over half of his feedings and the episodes of projectile vomiting and when you consider that Megan Eddy was in labor for thirty-nine hours, twenty-seven hours of which were after the membrane had broken which caused Roston's head while attempting to go through the birth canal and failing because of the failure to progress or dilate beyond five centimeters, and Roston's head was stuck and had to be guided to the incision site by Dr. Hall's hand - Does your common sense and life experiences tell you that Roston Hanson's skull was fractured in the birthing process?

If you have a reasonable doubt as to any one of the multiple elements of either charge you must acquit the defendant of that charge. The state's theory is that abuse of a child and a blunt force trauma occurred to Roston Hanson on April 7, 2015 by Kody Lee Hanson between 12:00 P.M. and 3:00 P.M. on that date only and during those three hours. I submit to you that none of the witnesses have established that Roston Hanson suffered a blunt force trauma or child abuse on April 7, 2015 as alleged by the State. Do you recall the testimony from Dr. Galaznik and others that there was no swelling of such size or fresh blood seen on the MRI of the skull fracture taken on April 8, 2015 at the Wesley Medical Center in Wichita to suggest that this was an acute injury? Not one witness can testify within a reasonable degree of medical certainty that there was a blunt force trauma that occurred to Roston Hanson on April 7, 2015.

What if this happened to you? Can I assume you would be offended by the lack of a complete and unbiased police investigation in this case and their misinforming the medical staff and those present at the April 10, 2010 staffing meeting about what Kody Hanson said during his second interrogation on April 8, 2015. You all saw the video tape and you heard what he said? In what world is it 'fair and impartial' that the prosecutors can infer and imply that the skull fracture noted during the CT Scan and MRI of Roston Hanson's head taken on April 8, 2015 at Wesley Hospital in Wichita was a fresh fracture, when the forensic pathologist never viewed the edges of the skull fracture under a microscope which is the only way to date the skull fracture? That was her job. She is a forensic pathologist assigned to conduct an autopsy and her job is to collect evidence from the autopsy and not to assume something and neglect to conduct a part of the autopsy because law enforcement has either lied or grossly mischaracterized what the defendant told them during his video-taped interrogation.

You all saw and heard the video-taped interrogation of my client Kody Lee Hanson. You saw the law enforcement officer tell Mr. Hanson that his son had a large skull fracture that occurred that day and further tell Mr. Hanson that the doctors were upstairs trying to save his son's life and they needed to know exactly what happened so they could treat Roston Hanson. You saw and heard what Kody Hanson told law enforcement of the only possible things was that when he placed Roston into the swing he may have hit his head on the hard plastic or when he was laying his son down on the floor, the carpet and mat and he was holding Roston's head with one hand and Roston's feet with the other that when Roston's feet were touching the ground he may have taken his supportive hand out from under Roston's head too soon and Roston's head may have hit the carpet and mat from a few inches. From this statement from Mr. Hanson, the police allegedly told a nurse working that night that Mr. Hanson admitted to throwing his son to the ground. Mr. Hanson never said such a thing, and the video tape interview shows that he never said such a thing.

Dr. Obeberst, when she sent the brain and other organs to Dr. Wiens, indicated in her cover letter dated May 28, 2015 that: "According to medical records, the father reportedly later stated that he had thrown the infant down on the ground." You also heard that on April 10, 2015 during a staffing meeting at Wesley Hospital on the death of Roston Hanson that either one of the two special agents of the Kansas Bureau of Investigation who were present told those present that Mr. Hanson had told investigators that he had grabbed his son by the center and slammed the baby down. Up over head and down.

You heard the KBI agents at the trial try to explain that this was just a statement on what might have happened to cause the skull fracture. But you also heard testimony from the social worker from the department of children and families who was participating in the staffing meeting by telephone and she said that she did not recall what she wrote down in her notes as being a possible explanation of what might have caused the skull fracture. – rather she heard that statement to be what Mr. Hanson had told investigators that he had done to his son.

Thank God that the attending physicians at Wesley Hospital ordered an MRI of Roston Hanson's head on April 8, 2015 because physicians who are familiar with diagnostic MRI films can view them and date an injury from an MRI. You heard the testimony of Dr. Galaznik concerning the MRI. You saw his power point presentation and heard his expert medical opinion that there was no new injury on April 7, 2015 as alleged by the State of Kansas.

Kody Lee Hanson has waited 610 days to tell his side of this story and you each heard it for the first time earlier today. You all heard the actual medical evidence to include the prolonged labor of over thirty-nine hours, twenty-seven hours of which were after Megan Eddy's membrane or in laymen's terms her water broke and how Roston Hanson was born with a birthing injury and how Roston Hanson suffered a stroke which damaged his brain in the womb, during birth or immediately after birth. You heard that St. Catherine's Hospital couldn't regulate Roston Hanson's temperature for over two days and how that is a sign of a brain injury.

How unfortunate that the investigating officers did not do their sworn jobs to fully investigate this case, to gather all the facts and potential evidence and to be through. Ask yourself why didn't the lead KBI special agent ever attempt to speak to the three physicians who were in attendance during the thirty-nine hours of Megan Eddy's labor or during the emergency C-Section surgical birth of Roston Hanson? Could it be that they had already jumped to the conclusion that Roston Hanson suffered a skull fracture on April 7, 2015 between 12:00 P.M. and 3:00 P.M. and that they had got a an admission from the defendant that he might of removed his supportive hand too quickly which they ended up reporting to a nurse he said he threw his son to the ground and later to the hospital staffing meeting concerning the death of Roston at the hospital, that he grabbed his son by the center and slammed the baby down up over head and down. These were at best grossly inaccurate interpretations of what Kody Hanson said during his videotaped interrogation and at worst, bold face lies! Thank God for the video-taped interrogation which you saw with your own eyes and heard with your own ears.

Thank God that Dr. Oeberst had the foresight to send Roston Hanson's brain and other organs to a neuropathologist, Dr. Wiens in Tulsa, Oklahoma. Without that physical evidence, we would be left with law enforcement interpretation of what they think occurred. Theirs was a rush to judgement that is not supported by the MRI test or Dr. Wiens' neuropathology report.

Do you remember on Tuesday November 29, 2016 when I asked you each if you would give more credibility to a witness just because they were a law enforcement officer? And whether you wouldn't automatically judge that witnesses' credibility differently than all other witnesses? I believe you now have the reason why I asked you all those questions. The prosecutor told you in her opening statement that this was a very simple case. Based upon the facts that the prosecutors were given by KBI Special Agents such a statement is understandable.

Law enforcement has an obligation to gather all the evidence notwithstanding whether it supports or helps the prosecution or whether it could exonerate a criminal defendant. It is not their job or right to pick and choose what evidence they collect. And when law enforcement does not do their job and conduct a complete and unbiased investigation and gather all relevant facts as they did not do in this case then it becomes the duty of the jury to render an appropriate verdict by finding that the state of Kansas has not met their burden of proof of each and every element beyond a reasonable doubt.

Ladies and gentlemen, I debated long and hard about whether or not to make very limited closing arguments. Please do not be angry with Kody Lee Hanson because I have taken even more of your time to argue about the facts, the evidence, and the total lack of a police effort to conduct a thorough and unbiased investigation or seek relevant facts or evidence. This is too important of a case for me not to recap what you heard. I do not mean to insult any one of your intelligence by not giving you credit for your ability to listen, take notes, and comprehend and decipher what occurred here.

If you believe that I have wasted your time by going over something or that I have attempted to over emphasize evidence or legal arguments from you as a body, I apologize. I was merely doing my job and representing Mr. Hanson who clearly appears to have been falsely accused of committing any crimes on April 7, 2015 between 12:00 P.M. and 3:00 P.M. as alleged by the State of Kansas once you now have all the evidence.

I would respectfully ask that when you go back into the jury room to deliberate that you look at the marked exhibits and recall the testimony you have heard. The State has wholly failed to establish that a crime was committed on April 7, 2015 between 12:00 P.M. and 3:00 P.M. by Kody Lee Hanson against his son Roston Hanson as alleged by the State of Kansas. It is not Kody Lee Hanson's job to show that he is innocent of the charges it is the burden of the State to show that he committed a crime beyond a reasonable doubt and I submit to you they fell well short of their burden and I would ask that you acquit Mr. Kody Lee Hanson after you deliberate and follow all the jury instructions.

I submit to you that if one or more of the twelve of you jurors find that the State of Kansas has failed to meet their burden of proof that Mr. Kody Lee Hanson committed a crime you will send a clear message to the State and to law enforcement that you will not allow the police and law enforcement to do a hap hazard investigation in any such case in the future. You will be sending a message to the police to do their jobs. The only result from such a message is beneficial to all persons to the police, to the prosecution, to all citizens and to any criminal defendants.

Ladies and gentlemen, I want you to look closely at defendant's exhibit No. 1 or A and the 345 pictures of Roston Hanson taken over the seventy-seven days of his life. Look at the way Kody Lee Hanson holds his son in those pictures and think back to how Kody Hanson explained to the law enforcement officers during his second interrogation on April 8, 2015 how he held or handled his son Kody Lee Hanson. What person who is alleged to be abusive would take so many photographs of their child (an average of 4 1/2 pictures every day of Roston's life) if they had anything to hide. Those pictures demonstrate that

Kody Lee Hanson was a good and proud father, that he loved his son, and that he never abused Roston as alleged by the State of Kansas.

Thank you for your attention and time all these eight days. Mr. Kody Lee Hanson and I know that you all have jobs, families, and other obligations and that you have given us eight days out of your life to ensure that Kody Lee Hanson is given a fair and impartial trial. For that we thank you and ask you to consider all of the evidence and testimony and then to acquit the defendant of these falsely accused charges which were made in a rush to judgment without conducting a necessary and through investigation of all the facts to include interviewing the doctors involved in the birth of Roston Hanson and interviewing the paternal grandfather and the fraternal uncle who both lost young children due to genetic shortcomings which would suggest that Kody Lee Hanson may carry a defective gene that was passed onto Roston Hanson, without deciding which information is important and which information is not important. Thank you."

## Chapter Fifteen:
### A Sign from the Sky Above

During the six hours the jury was back in the jury room deliberating on Kody Hanson's fate, I either sat with my client and his wife; by myself or with my youngest son. I also walked the courthouse floors to relieve my nervous tension. I recall about ten minutes before the bailiff came and got me and said the jury had a verdict and the trial judge wanted my client and me back in the courtroom I had been in the empty Clerk of the Court's office. I was standing near one of their windows thinking if there was something I missed or anything I could have done different, second guessing my preparation and efforts at trial. When I looked outside into the dark I saw a beautiful red sky highlighted by the lights from the business district of Jetmore, a small town in Western Kansas.

All at once I felt relief, and recalled how when I was growing up and old enough to speak, my father who was a naval officer during World War II, and a naval officer reservist for over thirty years after the war telling me anytime we saw a red sky the naval saying: "Red skies at night, sailor's delight - Red skies in the morning, sailors take warning." The saying meant that if there was a red sky at night, the weather would be fine the next morning and there shouldn't be a problem sailing the next day. The saying also meant that if there was a red sky in the morning that the weather was going to be a problem later that day and that sailing would be a problem. Over the years, I attributed a red sky at night to signal good things to come.

I also shared the saying that my father taught me and my two brothers with my wife, daughter, and two sons every time we saw a red sky at night or a red sky in the morning. I suspect that the red sky saying has become a three generational family saying and all of our grandchildren have also heard that saying from their parents in response to a red sky. It is not unusual for the Western Kansas sky to be red at night several times each year and less often to be red in the morning.

I recall smiling, looking back at the red sky, and looking up in the sky and saying, "Thanks Dad." I didn't know whether it was a sign from my father who I believed based on my faith was in heaven and he was somehow able to get a message to me to relieve my stress and to help me relieve the stress of Kody Hanson whose freedom was in the hands of twelve strangers.

Whoever it was that sent the sign, I believed then over five years ago that it was a sign from heaven, written in the sky above and still believe that today. At the very least, the red sky triggered fond memories of my father and had an immediate calming effect on me. I left the clerk's office and walked into the courtroom where my youngest son was sitting. He had graduated from law school two years before the trial and was my second chair at the trial.

I told my youngest son that I think it is going to be okay and that I believe his grandfather just sent a message to us not to worry. I explained that there was a red sky outside the clerk's window and he smiled. He got up from the table and walked outside the courtroom to the Clerk of the Court's office and looked at the bright red sky and returned to where I was sitting and he was still smiling. I felt like crying tears of joy and relief but I didn't want my youngest son, Kody Hanson, the audience members waiting in the courtroom for a verdict or the jury to see me cry. They all would however see me cry fifteen minutes later.

My youngest son had no problem believing that his grandfather sent us a message. My father, who was terminal, came from Idaho to live with us in Kansas for the last five months of his life with hospice involved and he died in our home from cancer at age eighty-seven. My youngest son who was twelve years old was the only child living at home at the time and he developed a strong bond with his grandfather and grandmother while they lived with us.

Several days after my father died my youngest son had a dream that he described as he was walking down the sidewalk in our small town in the rain and when he stopped to sit on a bench, there was a man sitting at the end of the bench with his back to him. The man turned and faced my youngest son, and it was his grandfather who held up his hand to wave to my youngest son and told him, "Bubba, don't worry everything is going to be all right." My youngest son still recalls his very vivid dream from twenty-three years ago.

My youngest son never had another dream about his grandfather that he shared with me. For a twelve-year-old boy to have that experience of watching his grandfather peacefully die in our home and then days later dreaming and seeing his grandfather in his dreams sitting on a bench and speaking to him to give him comfort was a beautiful thing for him and not an unpleasant or weird experience as one might think

I didn't share what I saw outside the Clerk of the Court's window in the sky and how I was interrupting it with Kody Hanson or anyone else other than my youngest son. There wasn't enough time because we had been called back into the courtroom. I was relieved after seeing the red sky until the bailiff came and told me the jury had a verdict and I knew the short several minute wait until the verdict was read by the Clerk of the Court would be some of the longest minutes of Kody Hanson's life.

# CHAPTER SIXTEEN:
## THE JURY'S VERDICT

I went and told Kody Hanson that we needed to get back into the courtroom because the jury had a verdict. For the next few minutes while waiting in the courtroom with Kody Hanson at the defense counsel's table for the bailiff to open the door and have the jury walk in a take their assigned jury seats, it seemed like an eternity.

I noted that almost all of the jurors had stoic and emotionless faces and didn't appear to look in the direction of either the defense table or the prosecution table - they just looked forward while walking to and taking their assigned seats. Some seasoned attorneys believe that if a juror when returning from the jury room with a verdict, walks towards their assigned juror chair and looks in your direction and smiles it is a good sign. I don't believe that and in all the years I had been involved with jury trials I never believed I could read a jury who was returning from the jury room with a verdict.

Once the jury was all seated, the judge asked the jury who was the foreperson and the last of the physician's assistants told the trial judge that he was the foreperson. I was pleased because I believed that a medical professional on the jury could answer any other juror's questions about the diagnostic tests; the medical records and the courtroom testimony from the various medical expert witnesses. The trial judge then asked the foreperson if the jury had reached a verdict and he answered they had. The trial judge then asked the foreperson to hand the completed verdict form to the Clerk of the Court.

The verdict form was the last page in multiple page jury instructions and allows the foreperson to check a box that either says we the jury find the defendant - guilty or a box that says we the jury find the defendant — not guilty on each of the two counts, murder and felony child abuse and it is then signed by the jury foreperson. The trial judge asked Kody Hanson to please stand, and he and I both stood up and faced the trial judge who then asked the Clerk of the Court to please read the jury's verdict. The Clerk of the Court read the verdict form that said the jury had found Kody Hanson not guilty on both counts of felony child abuse and murder.

On December 9, 2016, after nine full days of trial and six hours of deliberations and several written questions from the jury given to the bailiff for presentation to the trial judge, the Hodgeman County jury of twelve found Kody Hanson "not guilty" of the charges of felony child abuse and murder, filed by the Kansas Attorney General's Office against Kody Lee Hanson in the death of his seventy-seven day old son, Roston Hanson.

When the jury has a question of the trial judge during their deliberations, the jury foreperson is instructed to write the question out on a piece of paper and ring the bell which tells the court bailiff that the jury has a question. The bailiff then brings the written question to the trial judge who then has the bailiff get the prosecutors, defense counsel, and defendant to come back into the courtroom. A brief hearing is held outside the presence of the jury where the trial judge reads the jury's question aloud and the trial judge then allows counsel to make suggestions on how to answer the question, but ultimately the trial judge answers the question in writing and sends his answer back to the jury by giving it to the bailiff. A sample answer is usually: "In regard to your question, please refer to the jury instructions."

All discussions between the trial judge and the prosecutors and defense counsel are recorded by the same court reporter who records everything that has been said in the court from the voir dire process through the conclusion of the trial. If an appeal is later filed by either party, the court reporter transcribes the trial record from his or her recorded typed shorthand notes. When the Clerk of the Court read the not guilty verdict, I started to tear up with relief and anger. I was relieved that the jury had spent over six hours deliberating the evidence and the jury instructions and had spent nine days giving Kody Hanson a fair trial and acquitted him of both charges.

I was angry because none of those eight months of preparation for jury trial, the nine days of jury trial, or the six months that Kody Hanson spent in pre-trial confinement in jail; or all the costs and emotional trauma for Kody Hanson, his wife, and their families would have been necessary if the coroner had just done a complete autopsy and used histology and viewed the edges of the skull fracture under the microscope like she did with the other broken bones found during the provisional autopsy of Roston Hanson that she performed on April 9, 2015.

I was also angry because law enforcement investigators never conducted an exhaustive criminal investigation into how Roston suffered a skull fracture and they failed to have a radiologist trained in child trauma read the MRI diagnostic test to date the skull fracture. I was also angry because the law enforcement investigators either grossly mischaracterized what Kody Hanson said during his interrogation or outright lied about what they said that Kody Hanson had said during his audio and video-taped interrogation.

The trial judge asked the state and defense if we wanted the jury to be polled which means the trial judge asks each of the jury members if the not guilty verdict on both criminal charges read by the Clerk of the Court was their verdict. I believe both sides asked for the trial judge to poll the jury and the trial judge asked the jurors individually if their verdict was not guilty. The polling of the jury is a very important step in the jury process and I always ask the trial judge to poll the jury in every case. I recall in one of my criminal jury trials the Clerk of the Court misread the jury verdict form and said that the jury found the defendant guilty of the charge, when in reality the jury found the defendant not guilty of the charge and the jury verdict form reflected a not guilty verdict.

In that case, when the jury was being polled and the first juror was asked if the guilty verdict that the Clerk of the Court had just read was their verdict answered, "No," the trial judge asked the Clerk of the Court to hand him the verdict form and he noted that the Clerk of the Court had misread the verdict form. By this time in Kody Hanson's jury trial when the trial judge was polling the jury, I had visible tears in my eyes from the overwhelming relief I then felt and from tears of joy for Roston, Kody and Megan Hanson.

I turned and looked at my client and saw Kody Hanson was slumped over at the defense table bracing himself with his outstretched hands resting on the table and crying so I embraced him to comfort and congratulate him. Kody Hanson looked back in the courtroom where his wife was sitting and crying and Kody Hanson broke down crying tears of joy as I continued to embrace him. I watched the jury and saw they were focused on Kody Hanson and me embracing each other and some jurors appeared to have tears in their eyes. Each juror was asked by the trial judge if it was their verdict and they each answered that question from the court by saying, "Yes." As each juror said yes, I looked directly at them from the defense counsel's table and said, "Thank you." I started to notice that most jurors appeared to have some tears in their eyes as they each answered the court's question and a few jurors were openly crying.

Whether my client's tears of relief or their own relief caused the jurors to tear up I do not know. It all happened so fast. I do know that in all the years I participated in jury trials I never had such an emotional response myself and never saw such an emotional response to a verdict from a client and from a jury in the same case. Kody Hanson, his wife Megan Hanson and their families and I were all exhausted from the long stressful jury trial and were very relieved from the jury's verdict.

There was a lot of crying going on in that courtroom after the verdict was read and the jury was dismissed to go home. The crying I believe was relief and tears of joy that the American Jurisprudence system had worked as it was designed to work. Kody Hanson an innocent man had been set free of the false charges filed against him by the State of Kansas by a jury of his peers.

Normally after a jury trial, the trial judge asks the jury to remain in a room in the courthouse and allow the attorneys to ask them questions about their verdict and about what they could have done different. The jury had been working for nine full days over a two-week period, and it was almost 11:00 P.M. after a full day of trial and over six hours of deliberation. The trial judge didn't ask the jury to stay and speak with the attorneys. I clearly understood the trial judge's thought process in that situation. The trial judge thanked the jurors for their service and told the jury and all those present in the courtroom that this was the longest jury trial he had ever presided over in his legal career as a judge.

After my first several jury trials starting in 1984, I never stayed behind again and spoke to any jurors after any of my jury trials. Win or lose, I always send the jurors a generically worded but sincere and edited letter thanking them for giving my client a fair trial and for doing their civic duty. That letter says if they have any questions of me that they are free to contact me by telephone or letter. In thirty-two years of jury trials I never received a letter or call from any juror that I remember in response to my post jury trial letters sent to the jurors after each of my jury trials.

I did have a juror come up to me in a grocery store several days after a civil jury trial where I worked for a large law firm and we represented the plaintiff. That juror grabbed my hand and she said that she and one other juror had wanted to award our client more money than the jury ended up awarding the plaintiff. I thanked the juror for her kind words. As I recall back 34 years ago the plaintiff's verdict was sufficient and fair.

I had another juror who approached me in a bank several weeks after a criminal jury trial. When the juror approached me, I had my late best friend with me and when he heard that juror tell me that she thought she was seeing Matlock in action watching me at the trial, my best friend started calling me Matlock as a nickname after we left the bank. He called me that nickname for many years after until he passed away. I can't even watch reruns of Matlock now without smiling and thinking of my late best friend.

I also had the pleasure while I was still an active licensed attorney practicing law in Kansas of sitting and watching from the back of the courtroom where the audience sits and not from the defense counsel's table, each of my sons in one of their individual jury trials where they were court-appointed to represent a criminal defendant. I choose not to speak with the jurors after their jury trials because I wanted my sons to experience those unique question sessions with the jury members on their own. I had torn emotions. I wanted to share in my sons' victories as a proud father but chose instead to ask each of them at a later date what the jurors told them after their jury trials. Juries are a very important part of the American Jurisprudence system and our country is unique because we use juries to decide the guilt or inno-cence of a criminal defendant.

I will miss criminal defense work now that I am fully retired, but I will not miss the long hours. I told any young attorney that ever worked for me, to include both of my sons that it is much better to prepare too much than to not prepare enough. I told them you can always catch up on sleep after your jury trial ends, but it is near impossible to prepare for something you forget to do before the trial, during the middle of a trial, especially where many crim-inal defense trials can be tried in one or two days.

# Chapter Seventeen:
## Justice for Baby Roston

In 2018, Kody and Megan Hanson welcomed the birth of a healthy baby girl. In 2022, Kody and Megan Hanson also welcomed a healthy baby boy. Their baby girl and baby boy are true blessings and divine gifts from God in answer to their prayers to become parents again. While Kody and Megan Hanson's hearts still ache and always will from the loss of their son Roston, they realize that the birth of Roston's sister and the birth of Roston's brother culminated in justice for baby Roston. Kody and Megan Hanson cherish every minute of the second chances they have been granted to be parents again.

I believe from my faith that Roston Hanson even though at age seventy-seven days, he couldn't communicate, that he understood how he was injured during a difficult birth and the stroke he suffered either in the womb, during birth or immediately after birth. I also believe Roston felt justice was served for him and his parents, with the acquittal of his father who was wrongfully accused of child abuse and murder. That is the reason this book has been titled *Justice for Baby Roston*.

I recall asking the lead KBI investigator during my cross examination of him at the jury trial that if Roston was up in heaven sitting on Jesus's lap and somehow could speak or communicate with the lead KBI investigator from heaven, didn't he think Roston would tell him that he wants you to get this right? It is always a risk in any jury trial to ask any witness a question that you don't know what the witness's answer will be.

College students, law school students, and young lawyers at trial colleges and continuing legal education seminars are told by instructors to never ask a question you do not know the answer to during a jury trial. The example used is where a defense attorney is cross-examining a state's witness who had just testified for the prosecution that the defendant had bit off the ear of the victim in a bar fight. The defense attorney asks the prosecution's witness if he actually saw his client bite the ear off the victim and the witness says no. The defense attorney should have stopped there. The defense attorney feeling his oats then asks the witness another question he didn't already know the answer to. Well sir, if you didn't see my client bite the victim's ear off how do you know my client bit off the victim's ear? The witness answers because I saw him spit it out!

In Kody Hanson's trial, my question to the lead KBI investigator about whether he thought if Roston Hanson could communicate with him from Heaven did he think that Roston would tell the investigator that he wants him to get this right, was for the jury's benefit and I thought the investigator would give the answer he did. He said, "Yes," and I abandoned that line of questioning and moved on to other questions.

# CHAPTER EIGHTEEN:
## WHY I BECAME A CRIMINAL DEFENSE ATTORNEY AND WHY I WANTED TO WRITE THIS BOOK

As I was driving back to our house in Central Kansas after Kody Hanson's jury trial, I called the defense medical expert who had returned home to the State of Alabama after his testimony the day before and told him about the jury's verdict and thanked him again for his medical expertise and testimony. I then called my wife to tell her the trial was over and I would be back in Mississippi in a few days.

I thought about a lot of things during the hour while I was driving home in solitude. I wondered how many other parents, or caregivers had been falsely accused of child abuse and neglect and murder in the untimely and unexplained death of a baby in the United States. I recalled that 1,585 children to include Roston Hanson were reported by forty-nine states according to the data from the National Child Abuse and Neglect Data System (NCANDS) to have died in 2015 from neglect or child abuse.

I also wondered how many falsely accused parents or caregivers had been wrongfully convicted of child abuse and murder and whether a book discussing Roston Hanson's birth; short and traumatic life and death; and the arrest, prosecution, and acquittal of Kody Hanson which discusses birthing injuries, histology, diagnostic MRI testing to date skull fractures may cause some cases to be reopened and reinvestigated based upon post trial or other legal pleadings.

I decided that I should write a short book about what happened to Baby Roston and the arrest, prosecution on false charges and acquittal of Kody Hanson. I thought the book may help prosecutors, medical personnel at hospitals and medical clinics who are trained to recognize injuries from child abuse, coroners, and defense attorneys to consider in untimely and unexplained baby death cases the possibility that a birthing injury caused a baby's skull fracture rather than rushing to a conclusion that such injury was caused by neglect and child abuse.

I also thought that law students, and college students who were interested in becoming attorneys and were considering becoming a criminal defense attorney as a career goal and taking the Law School Admissions Test and then applying to law school could gain some real-life insight from such a book into what criminal defense involves and how rewarding it can be as a profession. I especially thought such a book could help falsely accused parents and caregivers. If the book only causes one person who has been wrongfully convicted to reopen their case or it keeps one person from being wrongfully accused of child abuse and murder in the future it will be worth it. I suspect that in the future the information contained in this book could have an impact on baby death case investigations and prosecutions in those cases where a baby's death is untimely and unexplained.

I wanted to wait enough time before I had the book published to allow for my full retirement and for Kody and Megan Hanson to have enough time to put this tragic chapter in their life behind them except for their fond memories of their son Roston who they were blessed to have as a part of their family for seventy-seven days. I also wanted to give the Kansas Attorney General's Office time to evaluate Roston Hanson's death case investigation and discuss the failures of the deputy coroner and law enforcement investigators in their State Child Death Review Board 2017 Annual Report (using 2015 Data), which is discussed below in chapter nineteen of this book.

When I think back on the fourteen year journey that brought me from leaving California in July, 1969 on a freight train that I boarded in a freight yard at the edge of the Mohave Desert in Edison, California to starting law school in August, 1982 at Washburn University of Topeka School of Law in Topeka, Kansas, I believe now that I was guided and steered towards becoming a criminal defense attorney by divine intervention since I was seventeen years old and homeless. He never stopped pursuing me.

I didn't graduate from law school until 1984 when I was thirty-three years old. Since graduating from law school and starting to practice law, I have always believed that I was called by divine appointment and encouraged in thoughts and dreams to concentrate on criminal defense and to allow BIDS and several judicial districts to court appoint me to represent criminal defendants facing serious felony charges throughout my entire legal career, in the same manner that ministers, school teachers and others with strong vocational preferences are called to their professions.

Each day as a criminal defense attorney, I thanked God that he never stopped pursuing me. "The spirit of the Sovereign Lord is on me, because the Lord has anointed me to proclaim good news to the poor. He has sent me to bind up the brokenhearted, to proclaim freedom for the captives and release from darkness for the prisoners..." (Isaiah 61:1-3) That was the reason that I continued to accept court-appointments to represent indigent defendants throughout my entire legal career.

When I finally walked away from the practice of law and retired effective June 30, 2021 one week before I turned seventy years old, I walked away as a happy and content man who was thankful to God that I was able to make a small difference and help some indigent defendants and their families as a court-appointed attorney over most of my entire legal career.

If I was granted one wish related to the legal system in general, I would wish that more seasoned criminal defense attorneys would allow courts and the Board of Indigent Defense Services in their states to place their names on the court appointment lists to accept court-appointment to represent indigent criminal defendants in the more serious criminal cases. Otherwise many attorneys accepting court-appointments will continue to be either recent law school graduates or seasoned attorneys with less experience in criminal defense cases.

I have always believed that every indigent criminal defendant is entitled to the same quality of competence and experience from their court appointed attorney that criminal defendants who hire legal representation receive from their attorneys, notwithstanding whether they could afford to hire legal representation. The money paid to court-appointed attorneys from the state is much less than attorneys receive from being retained by clients, or earn from practicing in other area of the law, but the satisfaction from helping indigent defendants by defending them in court in contested cases and helping negotiate reasonable and fair plea bargains in other criminal cases is very rewarding.

While many attorneys already do, if more seasoned criminal defense attorneys would agree to either represent one or more indigent criminal defendants on a pro bono basis each year or agree to have their names placed on judicial districts' Board of Indigent Defense Services lists in their states to accept court appointments to represent indigent criminal defendants in the more serious felony cases then the common stereotype belief from some members of society that all attorneys are greedy could be countered one case at a time.

Pro bono is a Latin phrase for professional work under taken voluntarily and without payment. The term typically refers to provision of legal services by legal professionals for people who are unable to afford them. All attorneys are encouraged to perform pro bono legal services when they first graduate from law school and many attorneys continue to perform these free legal services throughout their entire legal careers.

# Chapter Nineteen:
## The Kansas Attorney General's Office Publication

A review of the annual reporting of the Kansas Attorney General's Office publication entitled: State Child Death Review Board 2017 Annual Report (using 2015 Data) shows the failures of the KBI investigators and the Deputy Sedgwick County Coroner which prejudiced Kody Hanson and resulted in his wrongful arrest, his pretrial confinement, and his wrongful prosecution. In that publication, the Kansas Attorney General states in a prologue to Kansas citizens: "For almost a quarter of a century, dedicated professionals servicing on the State Child Death Review Board have worked diligently to review the causes of child death in our state. The Board is unique in its duties as it is the only entity in the State of Kansas that conducts a thorough review of each child death by analyzing medical records, law enforcement reports, social service histories, school records and other pertinent information including birth certificates, death certificates and autopsy records."

When the provisional and final autopsy of Roston Hanson was performed by the Deputy Sedgwick County Coroner, she was the coroner member, from the State Board of Healing Arts appointee on the Kansas State Child Death Review Board. The State Child Death Review Board 2017 Annual Report stated: "Of the fifteen deaths classified as undetermined by the Board, six did not have an adequate autopsy completed. In total, there were eleven child deaths in which the Kansas coroner or pathologist did not complete an autopsy or did not meet the minimum expectations for the autopsy." "The minimum expectations for autopsies on children ages birth to seventeen years with unexplained death suggests that in addition to a thorough investigation, an autopsy should include at a minimum, the following as appropriate for age and circumstances of each child at death: [1] Photographs of the child and of all external and pertinent internal injuries; [2] Evidence of therapy and resuscitation; [3] Radiographs for a complete survey of the skeletal structure, especially in children less than two years of age; [4] films should be reviewed by a radiologist or by physician experienced in child trauma whenever possible."

"Other cases revealed incomplete investigations or law enforcement agencies not being informed of the death. In some, autopsies were not performed or were incomplete, or toxicology testing of the victim was not performed." "The eleven cases below display instances in 2015 where the pathologist performing an autopsy did not follow the standards of practice." Hodgeman County, Kansas lists one under the category of "number of child deaths incompletely autopsied despite guidelines." That would have been Roston Hanson's April 9, 2015 provisional autopsy, conducted by the Sedgwick County Deputy Coroner, a member of the Kansas State Child Death Review Board in 2015 who failed to follow autopsy guidelines and use histology to view the edges of Roston Hanson's skull fracture to date the fracture and failed to review the MRI taken April 8, 2015 or have a radiologist experience in child trauma review the M.R.I., to date the skull fracture and to determine whether any injury occurred to Roston Hanson's skull on April 7, 2015 as alleged by the Kansas Attorney General prosecutors and the KBI investigators.

The State Child Death Review Board 2017 Annual Report contains the following statement at page forty-five of the publication: "Recommendation to Improve the Quality of Investigations in Child Death and Near Fatalities. 1) Improve the Quality of Law Enforcement Investigations for Infant Deaths. Law Enforcement should increase investigator's knowledge of child fatality investigations through high quality training including the adoption of the Center for Disease Control's Sudden Unexpected Infant Death Investigation (SUIDI) protocols, and the use of scene recreation and photography. Each year the SCDRB reviews deaths of infants in which law enforcement did not collect adequate information in the investigation for the Board to determine a cause of death."

# Chapter Twenty:
## Recommendations for Necessary Changes

1. Law Enforcement Investigators should keep an open mind and not jump to conclusions of guilt of a parent's alleged neglect or abuse of a child unless they have first conducted a complete and through criminal investigation of all possible causes of a baby's skull fracture found after a diagnostic CT scan, to determine whether or not the injury occurred on a date certain as alleged by law enforcement or if the skull fracture could be from a birthing injury or other cause.

2. Law Enforcement Investigators should determine whether or not a diagnostic MRI has been completed on a child's head where a CT scan reveals a large skull fracture and if one has not been completed, ask the treating physician to order a MRI diagnostic test on the infant's head to allow a radiologist experienced in child trauma to view the MRI diagnostic test to date the skull fracture to determine whether the skull fracture is an acute or current injury or is an old healing birthing injury.

3. Law Enforcement Investigators should review admitting records of any infant brought to a hospital for treatment and where there is a history of a prolonged labor they should collect the actual medical records of the infant's and mother's concerning the mother's labor and emergency C-section to determine whether or not the infant was born with a birthing injury such as cephalohematoma.

4. Law Enforcement Investigators should interview the OBGYN as a part of their criminal investigation in any case where neglect or child abuse is suspected and a skull fracture is observed on a baby's diagnostic CT scan and it is determined that there was a prolonged labor that lasted longer than twenty-four hours after the mother's membrane broke, the standard maximum time to perform an emergency C-section to avoid injury to the mother or injury to her child.

5. Law Enforcement Investigators in any case of suspected neglect or child abuse where an infant is found to have a skull fracture after a diagnostic CT scan should subpoena the actual medical records, to include the surgical nurse's inventory of surgical equipment used during any emergency C-section to determine whether or not forceps were used in the delivery of the baby and whether those records lists that the baby was born with a birthing injury.

6. Law Enforcement Investigators where medical personnel or other potential fact witnesses are refusing to be interviewed or questioned should subpoena those witnesses to appear and answer questions if there is an existing state statute such as the Kansas Statute K.S.A. 22-3101(1) that allows for a prosecutor to use an inquisition to gather facts and testimony needed for a complete and through criminal investigation into a baby death case.

7. State legislatures that have no statutes allowing for inquisitions should consider passing similar laws to the Kansas Statute K.S.A. 22-3101(1) to keep medical doctors from refusing to be interviewed and answer questions of law enforcement investigators in a baby death investigation, where it appears that the baby may have suffered a skull fracture during a difficult emergency C-section.

8. Law Enforcement Investigators and their supervisors should actually view and listen to any audio and video tape interrogation of a suspect or criminal defendant who is alleged by another law enforcement official to have made an incriminating statement during their interrogation, to confirm that the

investigator's statement about an alleged admission or acknowledgment by a suspect or defendant actually occurred as alleged.

9. The chief law enforcement investigator who is responsible for recommending criminal charges to state or county prosecutors based upon information provided to them by other law enforcement investigators concerning a suspect or criminal defendant's alleged incriminating statement or admission contained in an audio and video-taped interrogation should actually view that audio and video-taped interrogation to determine whether the reporting law enforcement investigator's characterization is accurate, prior to recommending to the prosecutors that criminal charges be brought based upon what another criminal investigator has told the chief law enforcement investigator what the parent had said during an interrogation.

10. Law Enforcement Investigators and other police officers should not be allowed to unilaterally "revoke the parental rights" of a parent suspected of neglect or child abuse and bar the parent from being present in his child's hospital room without an emergency court order, where a decision has been made by the other parent after consultation with the medical doctors to stop all artificial means of life support which will result in the baby's death, where law enforcement personnel can be present in the baby's room with the parent suspected of neglect and child abuse so that the innocent until proven guilty parent can be with his dying child at the time of his child's death.

11. Medical personnel trained to recognize child trauma should where a diagnostic CT scan shows a baby has a large skull fracture upon admission to a hospital, also order a diagnostic MRI test and have a radiologist experienced in child trauma read the MRI to date the skull fracture, especially where it has been alleged by law enforcement that the skull fracture occurred on the date the child was brought to the hospital emergency room.

12. States should consider enacting laws requiring medical doctors who perform emergency C-sections where the baby's head is lodged in a mother birth

canal and has to be pulled from the birth canal which results in the child being born with cephalohematoma, a birthing injury which may be an indication of a linear skull fracture and born with an elongated head, with an inability to regulate the infant's temperature, should have a diagnostic CT scan of the baby's skull taken to determine whether the infant has a skull fracture. Any such law should also direct that the medical doctors who order a diagnostic CT scan and find a skull fracture should then order a diagnostic MRI test so that the skull fracture can be dated by a radiologist experienced in child trauma.

13. Medical experts should be consulted to determine whether or not any infant who suffered a skull fracture during a difficult birth, who later aspirates while being fed formula and is resuscitated should be transported by ambulance or be flown in a fixed wing life watch airplane or life watch helicopter to a larger hospital since Roston Hanson was stabilized before being flown to the Wichita hospital and he suffered three seizures during his one hour life watch flight and died the next day which suggest that the cabin pressure of the fixed wing life-watch airplane may have aggravated Roston's already damaged brain which was damaged from a birthing injury, i.e. a stroke and during a difficult emergency C-section.

14. Forensic Pathologists or coroners who conduct a provisional autopsy on a baby who is found to have a large skull fracture should always use histology and view the edges of the skull fracture under a microscope to date the skull fracture and be required to sign a certification that histology was used, even when it has been reported to them by law enforcement investigators that the parent stated he threw his baby to the ground. This is especially important where other broken bones are found during the autopsy and viewed under the microscope by using histology and all the other injuries were found to be old or healing injuries and not acute injuries that occurred on the date that law enforcement has alleged the baby was subjected to neglect and child abuse.

15. Forensic Pathologists and coroners who conduct an autopsy on a baby who is found to have a skull fracture from a diagnostic CT scan and diagnostic MRI

should also engage the services of a neuropathologist to examine the brain, eyes, dura, and spinal cord of the baby to get a neuropathologist report to date all suspected injuries and any possible birthing injuries.

16. State legislatures should consider passing laws requiring that in any autopsy where law enforcement or medical personnel suspects that an individual is criminally responsible for the death of a baby, that in any autopsy performed by a forensic pathologist or coroner be audio and videotaped to preserve what was done and not done in the autopsy and that check lists be prepared to insure that histology is used to view the edges of a skull fracture under a microscope to date the injury in every autopsy of a baby who was found to have a skull fracture, and medical records establish that the baby was born with a birthing injury. These recording could be sealed but subject to subpoena and court authorization to allow attorneys representing criminal defendants charged with a crime as a result of the autopsy to discover potential exculpatory evidence.

17. Prosecutors should wait on the final results of a baby's autopsy to include any neuropathologist's report before bringing any criminal charges in cases that are contested and other potential causes are suspected, such as birthing injuries.

18. In any case where a local prosecutor files a recusal because the defendant is a law enforcement officer and works for the same employer as the local prosecutor, in those states that allow special prosecutors, consideration should be given to assigning a special prosecutor who is exempt from political pressure or ask the Federal Bureau of Investigation to investigate and the United States Attorney's office to prosecute the case if prosecution is necessary, rather than to assign the prosecution to the state's attorney general's office to allow a special prosecutor or the U.S. Attorney's office to have the discretion to decline to prosecute after a through criminal investigation or to dismiss the charges after exculpatory evidence such as a neuropathologist report is received stating that the baby did not suffer any injury on the specific date alleged by law enforcement investigators.

Otherwise, any state's elected Attorney General, the highest law enforcement official in any state, who is an elected official and a political being is unlikely to decline to prosecute or voluntarily dismiss the charges brought against a law enforcement officer where exculpatory evidence is received after charges have been brought for fear of negative publicity of any such decision to include claims or allegations that the chief law enforcement officer in any state is protecting a fellow law enforcement officer by not bringing charges or by dismissing charges against a law enforcement officer.